JESUS
MEETING

BRUCE MARCHIANO

HARVEST HOUSE PUBLISHERS
Eugene, Oregon 97402

Cover by Koechel Peterson & Associates, Minneapolis, Minnesota

MEETING JESUS
Formerly titled *Jesus*
Copyright © 2002 by Bruce Marchiano
Published by Harvest House Publishers
Eugene, Oregon 97402

Library of Congress Cataloging-in-Publication Data
Marchiano, Bruce.
    Meeting Jesus / Bruce Marchiano
        p. cm.
    ISBN 0-7369-0785-8
    1. Jesus Christ—Biography. I. Title.

BT301.2 .M28 2002
232.9'01—dc21
[B]   2001039809

Printed in the United States of America

02 03 04 05 06 07 08 09 10 / DC-MS / 10 9 8 7 6 5 4 3 2 1

Contents

From the Author

Meeting Jesus—are there two more simple, yet two more breathtaking words in the English language?

It's funny how that is. At the end of life's bells and whistles it's always the simple things that are most significant—in this case, *all* significant— *meeting Jesus.*

I remember meeting Jesus in 1989. I was working hard, an up-and-coming actor in Los Angeles, beginning to make headway after years of struggle. Lifelong dreams were beginning to feel as if they could actually be realized, and then suddenly—*whoosh!*—gone.

As wonderful as those dreams were, they were about as stable as boiling water. I called out to the living God. I asked Jesus into my heart. I met Him as Lord and Savior.

I'm sure that many of you could tell a similar story. Others, perhaps not. But the interesting thing—both for those who've met Jesus in this way and those who figure they've met Him enough to have decided not to—is this: As much as we've met Him, have we really *met* Him? As much as we know Him, do we really *know* Him?

That's what *Meeting Jesus* is all about—drawing us to that day alongside Him 2000 years ago...stepping out from theology and doctrinal complication and just looking into His eyes... peeking into His heart!

"And they will call him Immanuel—which means, 'God with us.'" It's a phrase we're familiar with, but can you imagine? He turns; He locks eyes with you—God in the flesh. He smiles; He moves toward you—the kingdom of God in the flesh. His hand, in all its strength, rests gently on your shoulder—the touch of God in the flesh.

Have you already "met" Jesus? Then come! Hear the trumpet call to worship echoing across the hills and valleys of ancient Israel. There's talk of a new prophet, you know—a carpenter from the town of Nazareth in Galilee. It is said He speaks with truth and acts with compassion such as no one has ever imagined before.

Have you not yet "met" Jesus? Then come! Stand in the temple courts with Him, share a meal by His campfire. Laugh with Him; weep with Him; look into His gaze; feel the sureness of His embrace; hear the whisper of His heart and glimpse the salvation of your very soul!

"Come to Me....I am gentle and humble in heart, and you will find rest for your soul." *Jesus!*

ONE

A Child Is Born

What kind of God would choose to be born in a barn—a barn in one of the tiniest little burgs in the ancient world? What kind of God would choose a peasant girl for His mother and a no-name blue-collar worker for His father? What kind of God would choose a feed trough as His first resting place, farm animals as His first companions?

We've done a good job of hiding the realities behind the romance of Christmas pageantry and celebration—all done, surely, with a heart to glorify the Lord we love so much. But to step away from those glittering nativity scenes, peel the poetry from those timeless carols, and stare into the face of unaltered, unglamorized, unreligionized truth is to look into the face and glimpse the pulsating heart of almighty God Himself.

What was it like that night 2000 years ago— what was it really like?

Think of Mary, this woman—possibly this girl—eight-plus months pregnant on the back of a donkey (if she and Joseph even had a donkey); dirt roads; mountain passes; sun, wind, cold; no shelter, no escape; just miles, miles, and more miles; pain, pain, and more pain.

Less than a year before, she had been surrounded by family, laughing with friends in the streets of her beloved Nazareth, a young woman betrothed to a gentle, godly man with a good trade, the whole world lying at her feet. And now, here she is, a nameless face in the throng of oppressed migration, trekking across merciless terrain, alone except for the kick in her belly, a man as worn as she is, and a promise that the tiny heartbeat within her is that of the Son of the Living God.

Think of the sweat dripping down her face, the trail-dust clinging to her clothes, the pregnant swell of her feet and limbs, the endless pounding of every step. Think of her curled up by the night's campfire, bundled against the cold, her mind and emotions racing: "Surely this is not the way a king is born into the world, let alone Messiah. This is not glory. This is not majesty. Did I hear the angel correctly? But I am pregnant, and there's no other way. It has to be true…help me, Lord, it hurts!"

Yes, I know we have greatly idealized Mary, but the truth is she was a woman—a woman with one tremendous asset: a heart after God. But she was a woman no less subject to the same doubt, confusion, fatigue, and fear as any other woman. A woman who had the same choice to make as any other woman: Am I going to walk this day God's way or my own? Am I going to trust Him—that He is who He says He is, and that His promises are true against all evidence to the contrary—or am I not?

And then there's her betrothed, Joseph. A man. Good-hearted, compassionate, and no doubt going through the same confusion as Mary, asking himself the very same questions.

Picture the two of them lying side by side next to that campfire, both shaking scared, both doing their best to hide it and be strong for the other. Imagine them having that standard exchange which has been going on between couples since the beginning of time: "Are you okay?" "Yeah, I'm fine." "Are you sure?" "No, really, I'm fine…How about you?" "Doin' just fine. Really…"

All humor aside, think of Joseph the man. His was a very real, day-by-day life 2000 years ago. We tend to overlook that in our hunt through the Gospels for great spiritual truth; we overlook the humanity, the dirt under the fingernails, the wrinkles on the forehead, the struggle to make ends meet. And in doing that we overlook what could possibly be the most significant truth of all: These were people 2000 years ago—very real, very human, very-much-like-you-and-I *people.*

And while they were "chosen" people, their chosenness had nothing to do with them being special people but everything to do with them being *yielded* people; chosen, not to live high and bask in God's favor, but chosen to serve (yes, this is the glory of God: to serve!), chosen to be a conduit through which the love of God and the plan of His salvation would flow, starting with the guy next door and to the very ends of the earth!

Try, for a moment, to put yourself in this man Joseph's shoes. Try to imagine that day he went home to his father and announced, "Mary's pregnant, but I'm going to marry her anyway because an angel told me the baby is Messiah!" Imagine, further, the day he announced it to his friends. I wasn't there, but I have to believe that each and every one of them looked straight at him and thought the exact same thought: *Joseph's gone nuts!*

You can almost hear his father exploding in a righteous rage, "Over my dead body, you'll marry her!" You can almost see his buddies sitting him down a bit more calmly—"I know she's a great girl and all, but the woman's pregnant, pal. How do you think she got that way? Open your eyes. Walk away."

And you know, Joseph's dad and buddies would have had every right to react that way, assuming that's the way they reacted. A woman pregnant out of wedlock! It would have been blatantly horrifying to their first-century culture, not to mention a crime so grievous under the law of Moses that it was punishable by death.

How could Yahweh possibly, in His ultimate holiness and purity, choose to birth His Messiah in such an apparently unholy and impure arena? To our oh-so-familiar-with-the-story hindsight, the incongruity rarely even crosses the mind, but to them on that day it would have made no sense whatsoever! It would have seemed an absolute contradiction of their understanding of the nature of God.

Picture Joseph sitting alone in his carpenter shop, mulling it all over. Maybe the day is done and the red sun is drooping low over the Galilean skyline. Mary arrives, as is her custom, with a skin of water and a fresh-baked loaf, but he's so distant today. She picks up a palm branch and begins sweeping up his wood shavings from the afternoon's labor. With all the gossip, there aren't as many shavings as there were two months ago. She notices, but says nothing.

He looks at her across the room. He wonders, "Did I hear God right? The whole town is laughing. They're taking their work to other craftsmen. She's so lovely. My father won't speak to me. My mother cries herself to sleep. Did I really hear God? Oh, God…"

But somehow he makes the right choice. He presses through, day by day. Against all odds, against all sense, against all opposition, he clings singularly to God's promise and as the days turn into months suddenly finds himself staring at the city gates of his ancestors—Bethlehem.

What a night that must have been for Joseph—his wife is going into labor, and he has no place for her to even rest, let alone give birth to her child. A guy would want so much to provide for his wife, to take care of her and cover her with security and comfort. But here's this man, and no matter how hard he tries, there's no room anywhere and no money to convince an innkeeper to make room. There's not even any compassion for his wife and baby—just a city full of slammed doors.

Can you imagine the frustration, the sense of failure? Here he is, facing his first big challenge as a husband, and he can't even put a roof over his wife's head. Can you imagine the questions racing through his mind: "This isn't going right! Where are You, God? Why aren't You providing? I'm just trying to do what You've asked me to do! Why are You making it so hard?"

In a last-ditch effort, he manages a stable, possibly a cave. Can you imagine his shame, looking into his wife's eyes, seeing her pain and discomfort as she lies in the dirt and straw, engulfed in the smell of livestock?

And suddenly it's not just her—it's this baby—this baby boy whom he has been told to name "God saves"—Jesus—because He "will save His people from their sins." This baby of whom the prophet Isaiah had written centuries before that a virgin would be with child and give birth to a son, and call Him "God with us"—Immanuel. This baby of whom he and his wife had been told just months before: "He will be great and will be called the Son of the Most High. The Lord God will give Him the throne of His father David, and He will reign over the house of Jacob forever; His kingdom will never end." *Jesus.*

Birthed in a barn, a place animals are birthed. A dubious palace for One who will reign over the house of Jacob.

Laid in a trough from which animals eat. A dubious throne for one who will be called the Son of the Most High, whose kingdom will never end. A dubious throne for God-with-us.

This is Messiah—King of kings, Lord of lords! Where's the splash? Where's the thunder? Where are the flashing white lights and jeweled mansions? Where's the glory?

This is My glory, My child: that I love you so much, I gave My Son—whom I love so much—to be made lower than the angels, to be made of no reputation, to be humbled, to be made nothing, for *you.*

A barn. A peasant girl. A feed trough. A carpenter's son. *For you.*

This is My glory, child. This is majesty. *Jesus!*

An Unlikely Start

Joseph, Mary, and the child would spend the years following that most magnificently anonymous night running from a king's raging jealousy. Barely out of the womb, and already it had begun.

> Herod...gave orders to kill all the boys
> in Bethlehem and its vicinity who were
> two years old and under.

Many mothers would cry in the streets as a result of those orders, their tears mixing in the dirt with the blood of their slaughtered babies.

> Then what was said through the
> prophet Jeremiah was fulfilled: "A voice
> is heard in Ramah, weeping and great
> mourning, Rachel weeping for her chil-
> dren and refusing to be comforted,
> because they are no more."

He was the Son of the Living God, and His first introduction to the humanity He had come to serve was murder, pride, fear, and agony. And so His first steps are taken, His first thoughts are formed, His first words are uttered as a refugee in the shadow of Egypt's pagan gods.

But eventually the jealous king would die, and the boy and his family would return to the friendly confines of the town His parents no doubt longed for and told stories of night after night. He would meet His cousins, His aunts and uncles, and when it came time for His king-training, He would not slip into a silken robe or take a golden scepter in His hand—no, that's not what this king or His kingdom was all about. Rather He would slip into a tattered and stained apron and take a hammer and chisel in hand.

The apron would be His royal robe, the hammer His scepter, and for the next 25 or more years, this insignificant little town, this carpenter shop, would be His royal court and kingdom.

> *And the child grew and became strong; He was filled with wisdom, and the grace of God was upon Him.*

> *"Sovereign Lord, as You have promised, You now dismiss Your servant in peace. For my eyes have seen Your salvation, which You have prepared in the sight of all people, a light for revelation to the Gentiles and for glory to Your people Israel."*

> —Simeon, on seeing the baby
> Jesus in the Temple

TWO

Repent! For the Kingdom of Heaven Is Near

They were words that had been sitting on the edge of His lips, tickling and teasing His tongue for decades, words He'd dreamed of proclaiming from the mountaintops and street corners of ancient Israel night after restless night: "Repent, for the kingdom of heaven is near!"

Once, when He was only 12, He stepped out. He sat in the temple courts among the most learned of the learned, astounding them to silence with wisdom and understanding not only beyond His own tender years, but beyond all they themselves had gleaned from their four or five or more decades of devotion to the law and prophets.

Little did they realize at the time, but all of their study, all of their feasts, all of their fasting, prayer, and sacrifice would be captured in that simple proclamation, that bottom-line essence: "Repent! For the kingdom of heaven is near!"

But in spite of the 12-year-old's unearthly wisdom, it was not yet His time. There were years—no, decades—of shaping and trying, of testing and forging. There was a perfection of timing, a perfection of obedience, a specific millisecond that had been ordained since the foundations of the universe, that had to be waited upon, and waited upon, and then waited upon some more.

There was a process, a pattern, a plan established in the heavenlies thousands of years earlier, before the dust of the earth below His growingly calloused feet was formed into tangible substance. "Repent, for the kingdom of heaven is near!"

But suddenly He was there, kissing His mother goodbye, packing a modest satchel, walking away from every companionship and security He'd ever known, trekking over mountain high and valley low and exploding like a rocket of magnificence from the muddy waters of a Jordan baptism:

> *"You are My Son whom I love; with You*
> *I am well pleased!"*

Finally, glory like we love glory! A voice splitting the heavens without reservation. The very Spirit of God Himself descending like a dove! High beyond high! Excitement beyond excitement! Majesty beyond majesty!

> *At once, the Spirit sent Him out into the*
> *desert…*

Forty days. It must have felt like 40 years. The pinnacle of His Holy Spirit baptism visitation, the laughter of distant family and friends, both ringing afresh in His heart, and suddenly there He is—alone. No food, no water, no shelter— alone. The same perfect will that spilled such glory upon Him yesterday now spills Him into the center of hell on earth today.

Cold, wind, sweat—and time. Time to think, time to reflect, time to long for the sweet warmth of His Nazareth yesterday and tremble at the ordained horror of His Golgotha tomorrow.

Time to hunger. Time to thirst. Time to shake against the frigid night and faint under the fur- nace day. Time to collapse at His Father's feet and cry out for something—anything—to eat, to drink, to shield, to protect, to give Him the strength to make it through the next day—no, the next hour, the next five minutes.

Oh, He could easily kick the ground beneath His feet and the sweetest spring of honey-water in all the universe would burst forth from the dry, cracked earth like a crystal fountain. He could easily take a stone in His blistered hand and with one thought transform it into the freshest of loaves, the choicest of meats. But...no. The Father says, "Wait, My Son. This is what I have for You today. Wait."

And so, against the scream of His every bodily cell and every human desire, He waits. He curls up at His Father's feet; He cries out for His

Father's strength—and He waits. And when given the opportunity to satisfy Himself and deny the humanity that would spit in His face just a few short years later and for generations upon generations, He looks earthly goodness in the face and through the sand wedged between His teeth triumphantly belts,

> "Away from Me, Satan! For it is written: 'Worship the Lord Your God, and serve Him only.'"

It was then that the devil left Him. It was then that the angels attended Him. It was then that His Father smiled a smile that engulfed the very cosmos and magnificently whispered what He'd longed to whisper for centuries upon centuries: "*Now!*"

> "Repent, for the kingdom of heaven is near!"

It's a message that ever-so-tragically carries the image of a crazed man on a street corner with a sandwich sign and megaphone. It's a message that is ever-so-misunderstood to speak of condemnation, judgment, Armageddon, and the wrath of almighty God.

But, praise God, nothing could be further from the truth. Repentance is not condemnation—it's liberation!

It's not judgment—it's joy! It's not Armageddon—it's new birth! It's not the crushing sneer of a wrathful God but an invitation to the party of parties, the excitement of excitements, the wedding banquet of wedding banquets— eternal life!

And it doesn't await some dark and ugly day of God's revenge, but "the kingdom of heaven is *near!*" It is now! It knocks at the door of your heart today and comes like a flood free for the asking!

I have to believe that when Jesus finally stood in some Galilean marketplace to unleash His streams of living water upon the world, He rose triumphantly to His feet, smiled a smile that would shame the sun, wiped the sweat free from His forehead, and exploded with all the holiness, joy, and majesty of the Man He unquestionably was—the Son of the Living God. "Repent, for the kingdom of heaven is near!" Translation: "Come and join the fun! Be free of all your sin! You don't have to live like you do for one more hour!"

Oh, what a marvelously magnificent day it must have been. And oh, what a shockingly ordinary day it must have been. I can't help but think of the people who shook their heads in disgust and walked past His invitation that morning. I can't help but think of the people who laughed to themselves and thought, "Here comes another one." And I can't help but think of Jesus at the campfire that night, tears in His eyes for His children so lost, so busy, so blindly and painfully burdened. He pulls His cloak up over His shoulder and lies down to sleep, accompanied only by a chorus of first-century crickets. His eyes open to gaze up at the wondrous heavens above, the star-speckled night sky that He and He alone knows was hand-hewn by His own design. *Jesus.*

Come morning, He would rise before dawn, make His way into town, and do it all again. He would stand in the same marketplace or sit in the same synagogue and speak the same invitation to the same people. He would not give up. No, He had been through so much already, and whether His heartcry would be heard by one or by hundreds of thousands, whether He would return to that campfire alone again or surrounded by multitudes, He was born for this very reason—for that one person—and He would rise to do it again, and again, and again—for that one:

> *"Repent, for the kingdom of heaven is near!"*

Well, eventually, one of those mornings, someone, somehow, heard those words in the depth of his or her heart and stopped. Maybe it was someone rushing to work in the fields or a child sitting next to dad in a donkey cart. Maybe it was a woman whose husband had just handed her a certificate of divorce or a crippled beggar lying helplessly in a puddle of street garbage.

Something tells me it was the latter—someone so utterly desperate, so terribly broken. Someone with nothing of this world to lean on, nothing to be proud of or claim as his own. Some devastated somebody who knew only one thing: "My life's a mess, and I need God."

It's always those kinds of people, isn't it? People whose hearts have been chafed raw, people who have been exhausted of earthly resource, stripped to dry bone, rejected and spit out by the things they trusted and a world that welcomes only the beautiful and successful.

But whoever it was, the day came, the heart opened, and the floodwaters of God's grace began to breathe new life into hungry souls across the land. And before long, Jesus would look around His once lonely campfire and see a ragtag team of unlikely faces lounging about, listening, questioning, doubting, wondering. A thief, a prostitute, a couple of fishermen. A man who would sit beneath His cross and watch Him die, and a man who would sell Him into that death for pocket change.

Though thousands would eventually come, these few would be his closest. John, Peter, Mary Magdalene, Nathanael, Andrew, Philip…a questionable gathering of absolute nobodies who, for reasons probably beyond their own grasp, had each turned their backs and walked away from every security they had built in life and every heart's desire that had filled their every dream.

Little did they realize that seemingly mindless decision—that decision their relatives and friends undoubtedly laughed at and scolded them for—would springboard them into the most remarkable, most privileged, most rare and extraordinary adventure in all of human experience: a day-by-day, side-by-side walk with the Son of the Living God.

Can you imagine it? Eavesdropping on the deepest secrets of the kingdom of heaven. Eyewitnessing wisdom and wonders inconceivable to the furthest stretches of human imagination. Partaking in the most significant events of all time—events ordained since before the beginning and chosen to be the vehicle by which the doors of relationship with Father God Himself would be unlatched and flung open forever and for all.

It would be their daily lot. For the next two, maybe three, years, they would travel through the towns and villages, over the hillsides and valleys of their tiny country, tasting what prophets and righteous men had longed to taste for hundreds and hundreds of years—*Jesus.*

They would sit at Jesus' feet in Jerusalem's temple courts and sleep at His shoulder in Judea's wilderness. They would share meals with Him on the shore of the Sea of Galilee and shed tears alongside Him in the streets of Bethsaida. They would gaze into His eyes, hang on the tenor of His voice, dance to the joy-song of His salvation, and watch Him single-handedly alter the course of universal history—forever and always, to eternity.

> *Land of Zebulun and land of Naphtali, the way to the sea, along the Jordan, Galilee of the Gentiles—The people living in darkness have seen a great light; on those living in the land of the shadow of death, a light has dawned.*

THREE

This Is My Son, in Whom I Am Well Pleased

How does one describe One who is utterly indescribable? How does one describe Jesus?

Hundreds of years before His infant cries first pierced the air of a Bethlehem stable, the city's most celebrated forefather, David, puts a prophetic pen to parchment—

> *You are the most excellent of men, and Your lips have been anointed with grace....Gird Your sword upon Your side, O Mighty One....In Your majesty ride forth victoriously in behalf of truth, humility, and righteousness....Therefore God, Your God, has set You above Your companions by anointing You with the oil of joy.*

Beneath his celebration of words, you can't help but sense what had to have been King David's overwhelming frustration—the awareness that as hard as he's tried, he hasn't even begun to approach the object of his poetry with so much as a whisper of justice. The totality, the immensity, the intensity, the intimacy—the absolute wonder of what the Holy Spirit has breathed into his understanding barely lifts its head against the constraint of human vocabulary.

Jesus: the "most excellent of men"; "riding forth on behalf of truth, humility, and righteousness"; "anointed with grace; anointed with joy."

Can you imagine the absolutely explosive human being He must have been? Think of His reality— here He is, walking among His creation, feeling between His divine toes the crackle and crunch of the earth His own hands formed in centuries past. He stands waist-deep in the Sea of Galilee. The wind He calls by name whips through the tangles of His own hair; the waves He set in motion slap against His bare chest.

I picture Him on the Mount of Olives as day breaks, exploding in wonder and dancing in praise to His Father at the grandeur of His own sun rising across the Judean horizon, celebrating the magnificence that He alone is aware of.

> *Therefore God, Your God, has set You above Your companions by anointing You with the oil of joy.*

He alone could understand the vastness of what His life would count for. His every step, every encounter, had been ordained from the beginning of time—every smile and every tear. His every conversation and relationship a pressing forward into the excitement of excitements: the salvation of His children and the indescribably miraculous triumph that that is.

Folklore and formality have done a good job of painting Jesus slight and solemn, distant and detached, of reducing Him to a long-faced, stained-glass image. But this was God in the flesh! This was all the bigness and power, the goodness and glory, the might and the majesty of the universe and then some, somehow incredibly wrapped up in the confines of a human body.

His were hands that had flung the stars into the sky, lips that had kissed the moon into being. He stood before the people and joyously proclaimed, "Before Abraham was born, I am!"

And now, here He is, living earthly life in earthly time. Walking among and living with the throngs of His most treasured, most valued, most beloved creation: *people.* Laughing with them, eating with them, working with them, crying over them. On a mission of redemptive love—the liberating of their lives into the salvation of their souls.

He alone knows the value of those souls, the value of their lives. He alone knows the priority that they are—such priority that the Son of the Living God gladly leaps from heavenly perfection and dives headlong into hellish destruction to save even one of them from the same fate.

He presses in with tireless fervor, marching forward with the confident stride of a man who knows what His life is all about, never once indulging a disappointment, never once wasting an opportunity, never once holding a regret or complaint or looking back. Just pressing in and pressing on, "riding forth victoriously" from town to town and life to life, bringing joy and healing, truth and liberty! And all for that one who would stop and be saved.

Can you imagine what it must have been like for the people 2000 years ago? To look into His eyes, to hear the belt of His voice, to feel the touch of His hand?

It would not have been a soft hand, you know. It would have been an experienced, calloused, thick-with-muscle hand. It would have been a hand that radiated strength, protection, bigness, tenderness.

It would have been a hand whose every touch was pure and giving, a hand that lifted, a hand that covered, a hand that cherished, a hand you just knew you could trust—and that whispered with its every touch, "I love you. I love you. I love you."

And then there was His voice. It would not necessarily have been the booming Shakespearean baritone of religious myth. He was God, and He most certainly would not have sought to establish His authority through such shallow attractions.

No, it was not tonal quality or oratory presence that gripped the people 2000 years ago, but passion…*urgency.*

You see, He alone knows the fullness of life that His Father promises, and the vastness of death in life that flows from simple lack of trusting Him. He alone sees the loneliness and brokenness behind the laughter and bravado, the self-destruction beneath the masks of "righteousness."

It floods through His physical, emotional, and spiritual senses like a tidal wave. It is His constant awareness—and so His heart breaks. It breaks into a million pieces, and His voice erupts in a volcano of compassion, pouring forth eternity-altering, uncontestable truth in a depth of heartcry that begs the people with every syllable of every word of every teaching and every parable, "Come to Me! Learn from Me! I'm gentle—I'm humble in heart! You'll find rest for your soul."

And then He turns, and from all the way across the marketplace or hillside, His welcoming eyes meet yours and silently breathe, "I know you. Mine are the hands that created you. They formed you while you were yet in your mother's womb—and I know you."

Yes, this truly was "the most excellent of men," and there would be little doubt the very second you laid eyes on Him. Explosively joyous, explosively alive, robust, hands-on, bigger-than-life, and as down-to-earth as it gets. The living definition of a hero.

It is astounding to consider—here was the Son of God, with all the power of heaven and earth and beyond at His fingertips, and what He chose to do with 100 percent of it, 100 percent of the time, was to give it away! Giving, giving, and then giving some more would be the core, the fountainhead, of all that He was and did—the source of His joy and the life-breath of His excellence.

It's true! As the Gospel records, Jesus never once used even the tiniest measure of His vastness of resource for Himself. It was always for other people. It was always to the honor of His Father and for the wellbeing of other people.

Think of it: He gives sight to a man blind from birth—He sleeps in the dirt, shivering against a campfire's embers. He feeds hungry thousands with a prayer of thanks—He sends His disciples into town to buy something to eat. He raises a little girl from the dead—He lays quietly on a piece of wood while a common man drives nails through His hands and feet.

Can you even begin to imagine the glory and excitement that bubbles within and flows out of a man like that? Free in His heart to give without inhibition or reserve! Can you even begin to fathom the love for people—love the apostle Paul terms "the most excellent way"—from which such choices cascade and cascade and cascade again?

> *Go back and report…what you hear and see: The blind receive sight, the lame walk, those who have leprosy are cured, the deaf hear, the dead are raised, and the good news is preached to the poor.*

Jesus just being Jesus.

How does one describe One who is utterly indescribable? Is there a word that means joy but is beyond incomprehensible joy? A word that encompasses the thunder of every waterfall, the dance of every brook, the laughter of every baby in the nestle of every daddy's arms?

Is there a word that means passion? A word that gathers the roar of every lion, the blast of every volcano, the peal and crash of every wave that ever exploded against a seashore?

Is there a word that means intimacy and warmth? A word that bottles the softness of every sunrise, the promise of every rainbow, the twinkle of every star, the tiptoe of every doe and fawn between every forest's autumn leaves?

Is there a word that means love? A word that means kindness? A word that means power, bigness, humility, purity?

I know of only one such word. It is the most awe-inspiring, breath-stealing, unequivocally magnificent word in this language or any other. Ironically it is a mere five letters, yet it carries a truth and meaning so big, so life-changing, so nation- and eternity-altering if only given the chance.

It is the word of words. The single word that every human life right along with its every human hope and struggle is answered by and resolved in. It is the beginning, and it is the end. It is the fullness of life, the gateway to eternity, the hope of the ages. It is…*Jesus*.

FOUR

Come to Me!

They came to Jesus as children 2000 years ago; made children by their diseases, their blindnesses, their poverties; by their twisted bodies, their desperate hearts, their empty purses, their hungry spirits. They came as children, and He healed them.

> Have you never read, "From the lips of children and infants You have ordained praise"?

It is a startling truth, crying out for its due from the pages of Scripture, crying over its abandonment by man. So quickly and so tragically we trade in our dirty knees and scraped elbows for combed hair and clean fingernails. Our tears before God become a suit coat and a study guide in the name of "spiritual maturity."

But the living Word of God as trumpeted from the lungs of the Son of the Living God is very clear in its cry: *This is what spiritual maturity is—*

Whoever humbles himself like this child is the greatest in the kingdom of heaven.

Unless you change and become like little children, you will never enter the kingdom of heaven.

And so, 2000 years ago, grasping that truth in the gut of her desperation, a grown woman crawls through the dirt, chasing the hem of a stranger's robe. A soldier kneels before the same stranger on behalf of a dying child. A thief scampers into the branches of a fig tree to catch a glimpse of Him passing by. A prostitute bathes His feet in the tears of her brokenness. A man blind from birth dances before the religious authority. A woman calls herself a dog as she pleads for an end to her daughter's pain. And all the host of heavenly glory leap for joy as their precious Lamb-upon-the-Throne dances on that throne and exclaims, *"Yes! For the kingdom of heaven belongs to such as these."*

One of the dangers of our familiarity with the events of Jesus' life and interactions is a jading to the raw realities of what really happened out there 2000 years ago, and who really was involved. As wonderful as all of the sermons and studies, the hymns and top-40 hits, the church plays and theological analyses are, in the quest for higher truth what very well could be the highest truth of all gets driven over: These were *real people* 2000 years ago. These were not caricatures or symbols or devices manipulated by God to teach future generations, but very real, very-much-like-you-and-me people.

The paralytic man whom Jesus healed 2000 years ago was not then "The Paralytic Man." He was a *man*—living, breathing, not unlike any man reading this page; full of hope for his life, dreams of a wife and family, and a thriving career at whatever trade or talent bubbled in his heart.

Assuming his body was not bent from birth, I think of him as a boy, perhaps sitting on the shore of Galilee watching the fishing boats come in as the sun limps low in the horizon, hearing the men sing and shout of their catches across each other's bow. "I want to fish," he whispers to himself. "I want to live my life on the sea. I want to be like them."

Or maybe he's walking hand-in-hand with his mother through the marketplace, spying the rare linens and exotic spices and seeing the finely adorned camels on whose backs goods were carried from distant lands. "I want to be a merchant." The boy's imagination soars. "I want to travel and taste the farthest kingdoms of the world."

And then comes the day when the boy's limbs dry and wither, his dreams along with them. I don't know what it was—an accident perhaps, a disease maybe—but his legs seized and turned to stone. They gave way to numbness, and with it went any hope in his first-century world of ever making a living, let alone feeling the sea-salt spray in his face or the far east wind skipping through the curls of his hair.

And so, in the imprisonment of a function-less body, his ambitions change. As he lies on his mat day after day, month and year after month and year, he dreams no longer of a prize-winning catch of fish but of his right hand somehow clutching a single chunk of fish, somehow lifting it to his mouth. Yes, his life's ambition has become to someday, some way, feed himself with his own hand.

He stares at the wall opposite him, and his imagination drifts not to lands far away but to the six steps it would take to cross the room and touch that wall. The tears he's shed night after night, thinking about that wall. Oh, what he'd give to just once touch that wall.

There are times when life gets reduced to its most basic. There are times when our fanciful pursuits, our grand visions, and our sophistica-tion explode in a puff of reality and we are faced, like that man, with wanting just one step, one hour without pain, one hand to hold, one piece of bread, one more breath to stay alive for one more second.

And so, like a child, the man begs anyone close enough to see the desperation in his tears, "Take me to Jesus."

Sweet desperation. The fervent prayer of a righteous man.

> *"Lord, help me!"*
> *"Lord! Have mercy on my son!"*
> *"If only I touch His cloak."*

Yes, it was in their desperation that Jesus met the people. For it is in that place where the sophisticate becomes a fool, the scholar becomes a student, the tough becomes tender, the elegant plead and beg, and the much-too-grown-up throws all of his polish and togetherness away for the simple heart *of a child.*

And standing among them, erupting in joy, Jesus thrusts His arms toward the heavens above and belts from the deepest recesses of His more-than-obvious divinity:

> *"I praise You, Father, Lord of heaven and earth, because You have hidden these things from the wise and learned, and revealed them to little children. Yes, Father, for this was Your good pleasure."*

Then He turns a sun-shaming smile to the paralytic man and everyone like him from 2000 years ago to today and tomorrow's tomorrow. He lifts the face, He wipes the tear, He looks deep into the eyes and breathes His peace: "Take heart,

daughter; take heart, son. Be freed from your suf-
fering."

Your sins are forgiven!

Yes, they came to Him in their pain; crawling
through the dirt, lying on a mat, begging in the
street; torn, rejected, used, afraid—they came,
and He healed them.

He reached a thick, gentle, divine hand right
into their wounds. He threw a warm, strong,
divine embrace around their naked shoulders. He
wept a thousand compassionate, divine tears over
their broken lives—*and He healed them.*

Can you imagine? He stops, turns from the
crowd, and looks right into your eyes—the Son
of the Living God. It's as if your heart and your
history lie bare before Him. The speech you'd prepared and rehearsed suddenly gets swallowed
beneath the tidal wave of acceptance that spills
from His gaze, and your lips mumble words so
simple, so unsophisticated, so gloriously childlike:
"Lord, if You are willing, You can make me clean."

Your face drops in shame at the sound of them;
tears leak from your eyes. *What could I possibly
have been thinking? He's the Son of God—what
could I possibly mean to Him?*

And immediately crushing that lie of lies, a
voice—tender and quivering in tears of its own,
in heartbreak over your heartbreak—unequivocally responds with the impossible, "I am willing.
Be clean."

It's *His* voice! Oh, yes! And it's *His* body that moves toward you and drops into the dirt beside you; *His* hand that reaches out and actually touches you; *His* love that explodes through your spirit, soul, and body, squalling up like a mighty wind and blasting away every tatter and tear, every compromise and confusion, every rejection and rebellion from yesterday and today to beyond the beyond. Glory to the Living God!

Yes, it is His love that makes Him stop everything He's doing; His love that makes Him turn all of His attention on you; His love that compels Him to reach into your wounds and cry for your loss and muster all the power of the universe to restore what was destroyed, redeem what was squandered, resurrect what was presumed dead. It is His love—His love for *you*.

And in the ecstasy of celebration that follows, far beyond the flesh that's miraculously pulsating with new life, far beyond the heart that's beating with new joy, is a bigger, more astounding thing—a life-altering revelation—that sets your feet to dancing and causes you to leap into His embrace and collapse into His arms and weep like a baby…"He loves me. He's the Son of the Living God, and He loves me."

> *It is true, my child. And there is nothing you can do to change that. I do love you—pure and simple.*

4 ⅈ

I am God— I gave My life for you; My life is for you; and I love you.

—Jesus

It is the mystery of mysteries, the reality of realities. It is the one constant, the solution to it all, clawing for air beneath the mudslide of human foolishness and self-seeking. It is the most precious, most maligned, most longed for, most fundamental, most pushed away, most sought after, most mistrusted, most cherished mystery/reality in all of human history: He is the Son of the Living God, and what He chooses to do with it is love *you*.

Whether it's giving His life in hanging from a tree or giving His life in the streets and market-places of ancient Judea, it's all the same thing: He loves you.

Whether it's bleeding from the wounds of three Roman spikes, or bleeding from the wounds of a heart pierced with compassion, it's all the same thing: He loves you.

There were many who were blind 2000 years ago; many who were crippled; many whose sons and daughters and fathers and brothers were demon-possessed or dead or languishing neck-deep in pits of the worst kind of poverty yet would choose that blindness, that lameness, that death rather than bend a single knee or shed a single tear in His presence.

You see, there is a blindness far worse than not being able to see. There is a paralysis far worse than legs that are bent and twisted. There is a death far beyond the tomb, a demon-possession far beyond fits of lunacy, a poverty far more devastating than starvation.

It is a disease that Jesus longed to heal and liberate His children from more than any other 2000 years ago, more than any other today. It is the filth of filths, the hell of hells. It is pride, self-righteousness, self-justification, self-pursuit, self-reliance.

And so, one priest calls Him a devil; another calls Him a bastard. A lawyer meets His offer of love with riddles. A wealthy man walks away. And the religious esteemed drag a helpless girl through the temple courts with rocks in their hands and murder in their hearts.

> *From that time on Jesus began to explain to His disciples that He must go to Jerusalem and suffer many things...*

FIVE

"O Jerusalem,
Jerusalem…"

~~~

He loved them as well, you know—the Pharisees, the Saducees, the religious authorities and
teachers of the law.

Many attacked Him. They challenged Him,
mocked Him, lied about Him, plotted against
Him, and did all they could to destroy Him. And
in our 2000-years-later-hindsight, how we hate
them for it.

But not Jesus. On that day, in the heat of the
battle, with the spit dripping down His face and
their laughter ringing in His ears, with the clothes
being torn from His back and the whip slicing
across His flesh, *oh, how He loved them* in the
midst of it.

It's an astounding truth—so astounding, some
would deny it.

But He is "no respecter of persons"; there is
"none righteous, no, not one"; and He came to
"seek and save what was lost," not push them
away. And in that, as mind-bending as it may

seem, the cry of His heart was exactly the same to the religious leaders—the men He knew would rejoice in the streets at the smell of His blood mixing with sand—as to anyone else: "Come to Me...and you will find rest for your souls."

When we think of Jesus coming to seek and save "the lost," we tend to envision drug addicts, prostitutes, convicts, and the like. But on a closer look, who could possibly be more lost than one who assumes, by virtue of his own righteousness, his own education, perhaps his own superior lifestyle, that he doesn't need to be found? Oh, the heartbreak of such lostness! Lostness beyond lostness.

And so these men, appointed...entrusted...by Father God to bless and shepherd His children, adorn themselves from head to toe in flamboyant displays of presumed holiness, strutting among the people like heaven's own peacocks, sitting proudly in the front-row seats of first-century Israel, pontificating and dissertating on what they thought was the law with such jot-and-tittle precision that they missed "The Law" completely, though they longed, probably more than anyone else, to look into His eyes and lay their crowns at His feet.

Well, they did look into His eyes. In fact, at 12 years old, slipping away from His father and mother and into the temple courts of Jerusalem, Jesus chose to go to them first. Some 20 years later, slipping away from Judea and into the synagogues of Galilee, He again went to them first.

And He would keep going to them. He would continue to reveal Himself to them. He would beg them to open their hearts. He would weep when they turned their backs. He would push the grief from His soul, pray for them from the depth of His compassion, wipe the exhaustion from His eyes, and go to them—again, and again, and again.

> *"I have shown you many great miracles from the Father. For which of these do you stone Me?"*

Yes, they would look into His eyes, day after day, month after month, for two, perhaps three, years. And what they would see in His every glance was His love for them, His heartbreak over them, His conviction of them.

And one day, on a hill named Golgotha, after all was said and done, they would get the chance to lay those crowns at His feet. They wouldn't be the crowns of gold they'd anticipated for generations upon generations, but then He wasn't the king they'd anticipated either.

It is a great mystery. If anyone should have recognized that Jesus was Messiah, it was these very men—the Pharisees and teachers of the law—who fought Him tooth and nail, and stood as His enemy every step of the way.

You see, they studied the Scriptures like no one else. They knew the messianic prophecies of old like no one else. They could quote it all backward and forward, inside out and upside down. They lived it and breathed it and begged Father God for it every day of their lives.

See, your king comes to you, gentle and riding on a donkey.

He had no beauty or majesty…He will not judge by what He sees with His eyes…but with righteousness He will judge the needy, with justice He will give decisions for the poor.

The spirit of the Lord will rest on Him.

Righteousness will be His belt and faithfulness the sash around His waist.

So there He was riding a donkey, the people hailing Him as king—and they missed it. There He was, sleeves rolled up, sporting nothing of human flash—and they missed it. There He was, in the dirt with the poor and needy—and they missed it. There He was, exploding with the Spirit of God—opening the eyes of the blind, lifting the dead from their graves, begging them with tears and confrontation to turn from their petty displays, to dive to their knees and from the bottom of their hearts crave *authentic* righteousness, *kingdom* faithfulness, and praise that comes from God, not men.

> *"Blind Pharisee! First clean the inside of the cup and dish, and then the outside also will be clean."*

But they missed it. Heartbreak of heartbreaks, they opted for stubborn pride despite the obvious, and missed it, and missed it, and kept right on missing it.

For with all of His true and evident magnificence—magnificence *of the heart*—Jesus just wasn't who they wanted Him to be. They wanted pageantry and splendor, worldly riches, earthly thrones, politics, rules, regulations.

In other words, they wanted Him to be like they were, and the fact that He wasn't—the fact that He was more interested in people than pomp, in goodness than glory; more interested in salvation than Sabbath, righteousness than rightness—was undoubtedly the greatest offense of all.

Despite who they thought Messiah would be, what stood in front of them was who Messiah *was*. What stood in front of them was simple love—love beyond love—feeding a hungry person, healing a broken life, resurrecting a tortured spirit. What stood in front of them was Jesus.

> *"If any of you has a sheep and it falls into*
> *a pit on the Sabbath, will you not...lift*
> *it out? How much more valuable is a*
> *man than a sheep?"*

Oh, a few of them would acknowledge His truth. A few would have their hearts pierced through the concrete layers of false expectation. One would even slip out beneath the cover of night and seek His counsel. Others would tiptoe from shadow to shadow and whisper to no one's ear, "Surely, this man is the Prophet."

But such utterance would easily give way to fear of man and be drowned in the deluge of self-accommodating folly: "This fellow is blaspheming!" "By the prince of demons...He drives out demons!"

And so their only salvation—the answer to all their prayers and their forefathers' prayers—collapses in the temple courts under the weight of having done everything He possibly could and sobs for the lostness of their souls.

Oh, what a day that must have been. With the sun barely breaching the city walls, the Savior enters Jerusalem, knowing the showdown that would take place, knowing the futility His passions would fall on and the cross they would lead Him to in but a few short days.

> *O Jerusalem, Jerusalem, you who kill*
> *the prophets and stone those sent to*
> *you, how often I have longed to gather*

*your children together, as a hen gathers
her chicks under her wings...*

*"Woe to you, teachers of the law and
Pharisees, you hypocrites!...How will
you escape being condemned to hell?...
For I tell you, you will not see Me again
until you say, 'Blessed is He who comes
in the name of the Lord.'"*

It was His last-ditch effort. From day one, He
had answered their every challenge, their every
question. He had reasoned with them, explained
Himself to them, loved them, invited them,
rebuked them. He had displayed all the wonders
of His Father's glory in front of their eyes time
and time again. He'd pled with them to know
Him and to know His Father, time and time
again.

But the Passover that would end all Passovers
was a mere two days away. The clock had all but
run out. Within 48 hours, those whose souls He'd
just wept for would assemble and plot their final
arrangements, thrusting Him into fulfillment of
the very prophecies they denied He was the fulfillment of.

*"But not during the Feast...or there
may be a riot among the people."*

One of His closest companions would assist
them in those "arrangements."

"What are you willing to give me if I hand Him over to you?"

One of His dearest friends would swear on oath that he never knew Him.

"Before the rooster crows, you will disown Me three times."

The thousands who'd praised Him just the day before would scream for His murder.

"Let His blood be on us and on our children!"

And being the Lamb bred to be slaughtered, He would hang between heaven and earth and perform His greatest miracle ever.

"The hour has come. Look, the Son of Man is betrayed into the hands of sinners."

SIX

He Is Worthy of Death

"He is worthy of death."

It was a simple, straightforward declaration, unmistakable in its intent. Five words, six syllables, 17 letters, given voice in the black of night as Jesus stood before the religious authority bound by chains He could have turned to powder with but a thought.

It was a declaration so incredibly, so blatantly, so obviously wrong—the fact that it was ever uttered is as astounding as Lazarus stepping out of his grave.

I often think of the man who dared to speak it. Undoubtedly, there had been times when he had wandered into the marketplace or sat in the synagogue, listening, watching. Undoubtedly, he'd seen Jesus in the dirt weeping tears for people's pain and recognized in the hope of his heart, *This has to be the Way.* Undoubtedly he'd heard Jesus speak words from the throne room of heaven itself and sensed in the pit of his gut, *This has to be the Truth.* Undoubtedly, he'd witnessed Jesus giving sight to dead eyes and breath to dead bones, and known in the very depth of his creation, *This Man has to be the Life!*

But unfathomably, in the face of all that and more, the words still leak from His mortally mistaken lips: "He is worthy of death." The words leak, and the horror begins.

> *"Many bulls surround Me; strong bulls of Bashan encircle Me. They hurl insults, shaking their heads."*

> *"The Lord looks down from heaven on the sons of men to see if there are any who understand, any who seek God."*

> *"But I am a worm and not a man."*

> *"Dogs have surrounded Me; a band of evil men has encircled Me, they have pierced My hands and My feet."*

> *"I am poured out like water..." "My bones are all out of joint..." "My tongue sticks to the roof of My mouth..." "My strength is dried up..." "My heart has turned to wax..." "My God, My God, why have You forsaken Me?"*

Blow by blow, lash by lash, lie by lie, nail by nail. Horror to end all horrors. The spit flew, the hammer fell, the blood flowed—and you and I were born again.

*"What shall I say? 'Father, save Me
from this hour'? No, it was for this very
reason I came to this hour."*

There are so many things I could try to say
here; adjectives, superlatives, graphic narrations
and analogies I could try to draw in an attempt
to somehow convey even a tiny sense of the realities Jesus swallowed that day 2000 years ago. The
trauma, the terror, the pain—voluminous,
incomprehensible pain.

It would be openly criminal for any one of us
ever to minimize it or filter it through rose-colored
glasses. Worse yet—tragedy of tragedies—to
mock it, reject it, or, God forbid, shrug a casual
shoulder at it.

My heart quakes to think of the passerby who
looked up into what was left of His face that day
and flippantly jested, "He trusts in the Lord; let
the Lord rescue him." History has recorded how
Jesus looked down from the cross and spoke,
"They do not know what they are doing." In the
case of this fellow, he knew not what he was
saying. Oh, how awful the day when it was
revealed to him. My heart also quakes for the
passerby who would look into Jesus' face today
and respond as carelessly, "Not interested." For
God so loved the world that He gave His Son, that
whoever would believe in Him would not perish
but have eternal life.

You see, there is the religion of the cross, the
intellectualization of the cross, the glamorization

of the cross, and even—it kills me to write the words—the debate over the cross. But clawing for air beneath the avalanche of all that and more is the reality—the *truth*—of the cross.

And that truth is this: Jesus—the Son of the Living God—a Man possessing all the power and ability in the universe to stop the horror anytime He wanted—chose not to consider Himself but to allow common men to tear the clothes off His back, spit in His face, drive nails through His limbs, and hang Him up to die in the afternoon sun.

And in the middle of it all, with a steady flow of blood twisting across His body and dripping off His toes into the sand beneath His feet, Jesus speaks words unfathomable, words eternal to those who looked on with their eyes that day and to us who look on with our hearts this day:

"Father, forgive them…"

You see, there is a way that seems right to a man—to take for oneself; to gather to oneself; to provide for, secure, and save oneself. And then there is the better way, the Jesus way, the way He chose to live every day of His life and every moment of His death: to give without regard for oneself; to provide for, secure, and ultimately, heroically, triumphantly, magnificently, save others— *at the cost of oneself.*

Why? Why would the Son of the Living God, who, if anyone deserved royal treatment in this life it was He, choose a path like that?

As the prophet Isaiah wrote centuries before a nondescript carpenter and his pregnant wife loaded up their donkey and journeyed toward Bethlehem, "He took up *our* infirmities…carried *our* sorrows…was pierced for *our* transgressions…was crushed for *our* iniquities."

In other words, because He loves you.

Not long ago I was reading chapter 12 of the Bible's book of Hebrews where it says, "For the joy set before Him, Jesus endured the cross." I'd read those words many times, but for some reason this particular day, it really caught me. I leaned back in my chair and thought, *What joy? What joy could there possibly have been in an awful, hell-ridden thing like that?*

I prayed and prayed, and after the longest time, words rose in my heart; words for me, words for you, words for everyone reading this page and beyond, for He has the same heart, the same hope, the same desire and passion for everyone and for all.

> **The joy set before Me was you. You are My joy.**
>
> **That the day would come when we would share sweet companionship, today, tomorrow, and for all eternity.**
>
> **It is you, My beloved. *It is you.***
>
> **—Jesus**

SEVEN

And Yet He Lives!

*"Why do you look for the living among
the dead?"*

His story would not end on that ugly mound
outside Jerusalem's wall that day. Quite the contrary, little did any among those who looked on—
those who laughed or those who cried—even
begin to suspect what was so humanly unsus-
pectable, so divinely foregone: *It was only just
beginning!*

Not that He hadn't made it completely clear
to them. Every warning He ever spoke of the
upcoming Golgotha was punctuated with the
remarkable and mysterious exclamation,

"But after three days…!"

Through it all, over and over, He pointed
their innocently confused faces to that third day
when the depth and enormity of the temporary
horror He'd marched willingly toward would be

swallowed whole by the eternal magnificence He was destined to soar into.

Can you imagine that moment—in the darkness of the tomb? Heaven's clock ticks past the last ordained second, and hell's jubilee is yanked to a screeching halt.

How does life reenter a corpse that's been dead for three days? What happens first? The spirit returns, the heart fills with blood, the nerves reattach, and the decayed tissues reconstruct cell by cell, molecule by molecule? The more one tries to figure it out, the more bafflingly miraculous it all becomes.

In my imagination, I see stillness, engulfing blackness…a blackness so black; and silence…a silence so silent…the silence of death.

The lifeless flesh lies straight and flat and still— so incredibly still. Then in suddenness beyond suddenness, with a sound like a megaton implosion of atmosphere rushing into a sealed vacuum, the chest heaves heavenward in one massive, back-arching thrust as the breath of life reenters and blasts anew, exploding through the lungs with all the resurrection force of heaven and earth!

Like a rush of flood waters ripping outward from the chest to the limbs, tissues snap awake, muscles slam to attention, veins pop and ripple, bulging hard against the skin.

The left hand tenses and grips, the right follows suit, and in one blindingly deft and monumentally sweeping motion, the body hoists itself erect and rises to its feet, arms thrusting skyward like two mighty pistons in an unbridled explosion of magnificence that surpasses magnificence, victory that redefines victory, joy like there never has been joy!

Throwing His head back like a stallion, hair whipping in a thick, black mane, He trumpets an unbridled, eternity-altering cry of laughter and praise to the Father, and the infinite legions of heaven's created and heaven's Creator leap and whirl and roar right along with Him: "He lives! He lives! He is Jesus, and *He lives!*"

Remarkably, throughout Galilee and Judea and all the ancient world it appeared to be a day much like any other, that third day. We'd like to think it wasn't—maybe an unseasonable wisp of spring dancing on the breeze, the sun rising with an unusual sparkle. We'd like to think there was "something in the air" that day—something everyone felt—a tension of expectancy perhaps.

But the truth be told, it was a day like any other, much like the day He was first born. Farmers rose early and dragged their plows into the fields. Children ran giggling through the streets and alleyways. Wives and mothers gathered at the river to scrub yesterday's dirt off of tomorrow's clothes. The marketplaces buzzed with merchants and villagers, the roadways with chariots and donkey carts. Chickens were bought, goats were sold, dinner was cooked—*and the Son of the Living God rose from the dead.*

There are so many mysteries revolving around it all. Why did no one recognize Him on sight? One of His dearest friends thought He was a gardener, and two of His disciples trekked miles alongside Him without a clue.

Why did He suddenly start walking through doors instead of knocking on them? Why did He still have the nail holes in His hands and the spear gash in His side? Why, why, why?

There have been a multitude of explanations and analyses, but the bottom line is the bottom line: No one really has the slightest idea. He is God, and who can fathom His ways?

But for me, the greatest mysteries are not so much those "spiritual" things, but more the practical, behavioral things. It astounds me, for example, that of all the "biggies" He could have first revealed Himself to—the apostles John or Peter, His mother—He chose one who was more than likely an ex-prostitute, Mary of the town of Magdala, a woman left out by the "righteous" ones, laughed at by the world.

It astounds me, the things He chose *not* to do. He didn't march up the stairs of the Roman governor's palace—the man who'd handed Him over to be killed—and call him out in front of the masses. He didn't pay the priests and teachers of the law the little visit they surely deserved. He didn't fly through the air surrounded by angels and land in the temple court and shout to the world, "I told you so!"

Instead, He quietly visited His family and friends. He talked to them and he showed them His wounds. He cooked for them, helped them in their work, assured them, counseled them, ate with them, pointed them to the future; and in keeping with every moment He'd spent with them in the previous couple of years, He quite simply and breathtakingly—loved them.

There would be no earthly hoopla. There would be no triumphant reception, no victory parade, no first-century press conference, no celebrations. Mysteriously, remarkably, shockingly, unfathomably, Jesus played it all in the exact same way He'd played everything that had gone before—that way that is so mind-bendingly opposite ours—subtle, simple, soft-spoken, gentle, guileless, low-key, forgiving, kind, backseat. *Jesus.*

And when He was confident they understood, certain they could stand on their own feet and march forward into the adventures He'd been preparing them for all along, He would leave them. He would tell them to no longer cling to Him but instead turn their hearts toward the next part of His Father's plan—His Spirit in theirs, filling them, cleansing them, equipping them, leading them, guiding them, loving them—being Him to them and for them, within them.

He would march them up a mountainside to a peak where they had probably sat at His feet countless times—these fishermen, thieves, prostitutes—these seeming nobodies. He would turn to them and share a final word: "Take what I've given you and change the world."

He would look each of them deeply in the soul—one long, last look. He would smile at each of them deeply in their hearts—one huge, loving smile. He would lift His gaze toward His Father, and before their very eyes, He would disappear behind the clouds and into the eternity from which He most assuredly came.

> *Peace I leave with you; My peace I give you...Do not let your hearts be troubled and do not be afraid.*

> *Remain in My love. And surely I am with you always,* to the very end of the age.

EIGHT

Meeting Jesus

I can't imagine that any work with regard to Jesus would be complete without a summons to that which was what He and His life, His death, and His resurrection, were all about.

It is astounding, the choices of the Son of God. He stepped out of heavenly splendor and relinquished His every right as deity to assume the posture of an ordinary man; to walk among us and work with us; to taste our sorrows and celebrate our joys; to instruct us, lead us, heal us, reveal His Father's heart for us, and more than anything else, to die, opening the gateways of heaven to us.

And the big question about it all—the revelation question—is *why*? Why would the Son of the Living God, with all the options in the universe, make those kinds of choices?

I've answered that question many times in the preceeding pages. But it is so huge an answer— so desperately vital to grip and grasp and cling to and never let go of—that as much as I've said it and as much as you've probably heard it, it just can't be said or heard enough:

He loves you.

Just as you are, whoever you are, wherever you are—

He loves you.

You see, the Word of God is very clear: "All have sinned and fall short of the glory of God" (that means you and I and everyone else are exactly the same), and "the wages of sin is death." In dying as He did, Jesus paid those wages for you and for me, for all eternity. He offers that to us—to accept His self-sacrifice as full payment, free of charge, free for the asking, the free gift of eternal life.

And so my question to you is, have you received this gift? Only you and He know, and if you haven't, I can promise you that He's offering it to you in the privacy of your own heart right now as you read these words.

Jesus said, "Here I am! I stand at the door and knock." Is He knocking on the door of your heart? Won't you let Him in?

> *Come to Me, all you who are weary and burdened, and I will give you rest.*
>
> *Take My yoke upon you and learn from Me; for I am gentle and humble in heart, and you will find rest for your souls.*

If your answer is yes, then simply ask Him—right now, right where you are: "Jesus, I hear You knocking. I don't understand it all in my head, but deep inside me I know it's all true. Come into my heart." It will be the beginning of a fine relationship—I guarantee it—and so much more than that, so does He.

If your answer is no, please understand He's a true gentleman. He doesn't ever force Himself on anyone, He just keeps right on knocking: "I love you, I love you…"

But you know, chances are good that sometime in your life you've already answered that knock. Whatever or wherever, you've done it and you're launched into a life of salvation in Jesus Christ. That's such a wondrous opportunity—an opportunity never to be taken for granted, or considered casually, or allowed to be fogged over by the "stuff " of life and its preoccupying pursuits.

Count the cost every day, brother; every day, sister—His cost. And don't ever for one second allow your salvation and your relationship with Him to become "just one more thing," or, God forbid, not enough to satisfy. Because when all is said and done, on the other side of all that we labor over and rush after and allow ourselves to get tangled in, every one of us will quickly discover *He* is the only thing—the big-time thing—Jesus.

So let us invest our lives wisely. Tomorrow never comes. Let us shake free of the superfluous and "fix our eyes on Jesus." He is the author and finisher of our faith, our perfector. Let us "consider Him," as He gave so very, very much—all that He is as God—in considering you and me.

> *Come to Me, all you who are weary and burdened, and I will give you rest.*
>
> *Take My yoke upon you and learn from Me; for I am gentle and humble in heart, and you will find rest for your souls.*
>
> *Jesus*

The Gospel of John

1

In the beginning was the Word, and the Word was with God, and the Word was God. [2]He was with God in the beginning.

[3]Through him all things were made; without him nothing was made that has been made. [4]In him was life, and that life was the light of men. [5]The light shines in the darkness, but the darkness has not understood it.

[6]There came a man who was sent from God; his name was John. [7]He came as a witness to testify concerning that light, so that through him all men might believe. [8]He himself was not the light; he came only as a witness to the light. [9]The true light that gives light to every man was coming into the world.

[10]He was in the world, and though the world was made through him, the world did not recognize him. [11]He came to that which was his own, but his own did not receive him. [12]Yet to all who received him, to those who believed in his name, he gave the right to become children of God— [13]children born not of natural descent, nor of human decision or a husband's will, but born of God.

[14]The Word became flesh and made his dwelling among us. We have seen his glory, the glory of the One and Only, who came from the Father, full of grace and truth.

[15]John testifies concerning him. He cries out, saying, "This was he of whom I said, 'He who comes after me has surpassed me because he was before me.'" [16]From the fullness of his grace we have all received one blessing after another. [17]For the law was given through Moses; grace and truth came through Jesus Christ. [18]No one has ever seen God, but God the One and Only, who is at the Father's side, has made him known.

[19]Now this was John's testimony when the Jews of Jerusalem sent priests and Levites to ask him who he was. [20]He did not fail to confess, but confessed freely, "I am not the Christ."

[21]They asked him, "Then who are you? Are you Elijah?"

He said, "I am not."

"Are you the Prophet?"

He answered, "No."

[22]Finally they said, "Who are you? Give us an answer to take back to those who sent us. What do you say about yourself?"

[23]John replied in the words of Isaiah the prophet, "I am the voice of one calling in the desert, 'Make straight the way for the Lord.'"

[24]Now some Pharisees who had been sent [25]questioned him, "Why then do you baptize if you are not the Christ, nor Elijah, nor the Prophet?"

[26]"I baptize with water," John replied, "but among you stands one you do not know. [27]He is the one who comes after me, the thongs of whose sandals I am not worthy to untie."

²⁸This all happened at Bethany on the other side of the Jordan, where John was baptizing.

²⁹The next day John saw Jesus coming toward him and said, "Look, the Lamb of God, who takes away the sin of the world! ³⁰This is the one I meant when I said, 'A man who comes after me has surpassed me because he was before me.' ³¹I myself did not know him, but the reason I came baptizing with water was that he might be revealed to Israel."

³²Then John gave this testimony: "I saw the Spirit come down from heaven as a dove and remain on him. ³³I would not have known him, except that the one who sent me to baptize with water told me, 'The man on whom you see the Spirit come down and remain is he who will baptize with the Holy Spirit.' ³⁴I have seen and I testify that this is the Son of God."

³⁵The next day John was there again with two of his disciples. ³⁶When he saw Jesus passing by, he said, "Look, the Lamb of God!"

³⁷When the two disciples heard him say this, they followed Jesus. ³⁸Turning around, Jesus saw them following and asked, "What do you want?"

They said, "Rabbi" (which means Teacher), "where are you staying?"

³⁹"Come," he replied, "and you will see."

So they went and saw where he was staying, and spent that day with him. It was about the tenth hour.

⁴⁰Andrew, Simon Peter's brother, was one of the two who heard what John had said and who had followed Jesus. ⁴¹The first thing Andrew did was to find his brother Simon and tell him, "We have found the Messiah" (that is, the Christ). ⁴²And he brought him to Jesus.

Jesus looked at him and said, "You are Simon son of John. You will be called Cephas" (which, when translated, is Peter).

⁴³ The next day Jesus decided to leave for Galilee. Finding Philip, he said to him, "Follow me."

⁴⁴ Philip, like Andrew and Peter, was from the town of Bethsaida. ⁴⁵ Philip found Nathanael and told him, "We have found the one Moses wrote about in the Law, and about whom the prophets also wrote—Jesus of Nazareth, the son of Joseph."

⁴⁶ "Nazareth! Can anything good come from there?" Nathanael asked.

"Come and see," said Philip.

⁴⁷ When Jesus saw Nathanael approaching, he said of him, "Here is a true Israelite, in whom there is nothing false."

⁴⁸ "How do you know me?" Nathanael asked.

Jesus answered, "I saw you while you were still under the fig tree before Philip called you."

⁴⁹ Then Nathanael declared, "Rabbi, you are the Son of God; you are the King of Israel."

⁵⁰ Jesus said, "You believe because I told you I saw you under the fig tree. You shall see greater things than that." ⁵¹ He then added, "I tell you the truth, you shall see heaven open, and the angels of God ascending and descending on the Son of Man."

2

On the third day a wedding took place at Cana in Galilee. Jesus' mother was there, ² and Jesus and his disciples had also been invited to the wedding. ³ When the wine was gone, Jesus' mother said to him, "They have no more wine."

⁴ "Dear woman, why do you involve me?" Jesus replied. "My time has not yet come."

⁵ His mother said to the servants, "Do whatever he tells you."

⁶Nearby stood six stone water jars, the kind used by the Jews for ceremonial washing, each holding from twenty to thirty gallons.

⁷Jesus said to the servants, "Fill the jars with water"; so they filled them to the brim.

⁸Then he told them, "Now draw some out and take it to the master of the banquet."

They did so, ⁹and the master of the banquet tasted the water that had been turned into wine. He did not realize where it had come from, though the servants who had drawn the water knew. Then he called the bridegroom aside ¹⁰and said, "Everyone brings out the choice wine first and then the cheaper wine after the guests have had too much to drink; but you have saved the best till now."

¹¹This, the first of his miraculous signs, Jesus performed at Cana in Galilee. He thus revealed his glory, and his disciples put their faith in him.

¹²After this he went down to Capernaum with his mother and brothers and his disciples. There they stayed for a few days.

¹³When it was almost time for the Jewish Passover, Jesus went up to Jerusalem. ¹⁴In the temple courts he found men selling cattle, sheep and doves, and others sitting at tables exchanging money. ¹⁵So he made a whip out of cords, and drove all from the temple area, both sheep and cattle; he scattered the coins of the money changers and overturned their tables. ¹⁶To those who sold doves he said, "Get these out of here! How dare you turn my Father's house into a market!"

¹⁷His disciples remembered that it is written: "Zeal for your house will consume me."

¹⁸Then the Jews demanded of him, "What miraculous sign can you show us to prove your authority to do all this?"

¹⁹Jesus answered them, "Destroy this temple, and I will raise it again in three days."

²⁰The Jews replied, "It has taken forty-six years to build this temple, and you are going to raise it in three days?" ²¹But the temple he had spoken of was his body. ²²After he was raised from the dead, his disciples recalled what he had said. Then they believed the Scripture and the words that Jesus had spoken.

²³Now while he was in Jerusalem at the Passover Feast, many people saw the miraculous signs he was doing and believed in his name. ²⁴But Jesus would not entrust himself to them, for he knew all men. ²⁵He did not need man's testimony about man, for he knew what was in a man.

3

Now there was a man of the Pharisees named Nicodemus, a member of the Jewish ruling council. ²He came to Jesus at night and said, "Rabbi, we know you are a teacher who has come from God. For no one could perform the miraculous signs you are doing if God were not with him."

³In reply Jesus declared, "I tell you the truth, no one can see the kingdom of God unless he is born again."

⁴"How can a man be born when he is old?" Nicodemus asked. "Surely he cannot enter a second time into his mother's womb to be born!"

⁵Jesus answered, "I tell you the truth, no one can enter the kingdom of God unless he is born of water and the Spirit. ⁶Flesh gives birth to flesh, but the Spirit gives birth to spirit. ⁷You should not be surprised at my saying, 'You must be born again.' ⁸The wind blows wherever it pleases. You hear its sound, but you cannot tell where it comes from or where it is going. So it is with everyone born of the Spirit."

[9]"How can this be?" Nicodemus asked.

[10]"You are Israel's teacher," said Jesus, "and do you not understand these things? [11]I tell you the truth, we speak of what we know, and we testify to what we have seen, but still you people do not accept our testimony. [12]I have spoken to you of earthly things and you do not believe; how then will you believe if I speak of heavenly things? [13]No one has ever gone into heaven except the one who came from heaven—the Son of Man. [14]Just as Moses lifted up the snake in the desert, so the Son of Man must be lifted up, [15]that everyone who believes in him may have eternal life.

[16]"For God so loved the world that he gave his one and only Son, that whoever believes in him shall not perish but have eternal life. [17]For God did not send his Son into the world to condemn the world, but to save the world through him. [18]Whoever believes in him is not condemned, but whoever does not believe stands condemned already because he has not believed in the name of God's one and only Son. [19]This is the verdict: Light has come into the world, but men loved darkness instead of light because their deeds were evil. [20]Everyone who does evil hates the light, and will not come into the light for fear that his deeds will be exposed. [21]But whoever lives by the truth comes into the light, so that it may be seen plainly that what he has done has been done through God."

[22]After this, Jesus and his disciples went out into the Judean countryside, where he spent some time with them, and baptized. [23]Now John also was baptizing at Aenon near Salim, because there was plenty of water, and people were constantly coming to be baptized. [24](This was before John was put in prison.) [25]An argument developed between some of John's disciples and a certain Jew over the matter of ceremonial washing. [26]They came to John

and said to him, "Rabbi, that man who was with you on the other side of the Jordan—the one you testified about—well, he is baptizing, and everyone is going to him."

27To this John replied, "A man can receive only what is given him from heaven. 28You yourselves can testify that I said, 'I am not the Christ but am sent ahead of him.' 29The bride belongs to the bridegroom. The friend who attends the bridegroom waits and listens for him, and is full of joy when he hears the bridegroom's voice. That joy is mine, and it is now complete. 30He must become greater; I must become less.

31"The one who comes from above is above all; the one who is from the earth belongs to the earth, and speaks as one from the earth. The one who comes from heaven is above all. 32He testifies to what he has seen and heard, but no one accepts his testimony. 33The man who has accepted it has certified that God is truthful. 34For the one whom God has sent speaks the words of God, for God gives the Spirit without limit. 35The Father loves the Son and has placed everything in his hands. 36Whoever believes in the Son has eternal life, but whoever rejects the Son will not see life, for God's wrath remains on him."

4

The Pharisees heard that Jesus was gaining and baptizing more disciples than John, 2although in fact it was not Jesus who baptized, but his disciples. 3When the Lord learned of this, he left Judea and went back once more to Galilee.

4Now he had to go through Samaria. 5So he came to a town in Samaria called Sychar, near the plot of ground Jacob had given to his son Joseph. 6Jacob's well was there, and Jesus, tired as he was from the journey, sat down by the well. It was about the sixth hour.

[7]When a Samaritan woman came to draw water, Jesus said to her, "Will you give me a drink?" [8](His disciples had gone into the town to buy food.)

[9]The Samaritan woman said to him, "You are a Jew and I am a Samaritan woman. How can you ask me for a drink?" (For Jews do not associate with Samaritans.)

[10]Jesus answered her, "If you knew the gift of God and who it is that asks you for a drink, you would have asked him and he would have given you living water."

[11]"Sir," the woman said, "you have nothing to draw with and the well is deep. Where can you get this living water? [12]Are you greater than our father Jacob, who gave us the well and drank from it himself, as did also his sons and his flocks and herds?"

[13]Jesus answered, "Everyone who drinks this water will be thirsty again, [14]but whoever drinks the water I give him will never thirst. Indeed, the water I give him will become in him a spring of water welling up to eternal life."

[15]The woman said to him, "Sir, give me this water so that I won't get thirsty and have to keep coming here to draw water."

[16]He told her, "Go, call your husband and come back."

[17]"I have no husband," she replied.

Jesus said to her, "You are right when you say you have no husband. [18]The fact is, you have had five husbands, and the man you now have is not your husband. What you have just said is quite true."

[19]"Sir," the woman said, "I can see that you are a prophet. [20]Our fathers worshiped on this mountain, but you Jews claim that the place where we must worship is in Jerusalem."

²¹Jesus declared, "Believe me, woman, a time is coming when you will worship the Father neither on this mountain nor in Jerusalem. ²²You Samaritans worship what you do not know; we worship what we do know, for salvation is from the Jews. ²³Yet a time is coming and has now come when the true worshipers will worship the Father in spirit and truth, for they are the kind of worshipers the Father seeks. ²⁴God is spirit, and his worshipers must worship in spirit and in truth."

²⁵The woman said, "I know that Messiah" (called Christ) "is coming. When he comes, he will explain everything to us."

²⁶Then Jesus declared, "I who speak to you am he."

²⁷Just then his disciples returned and were surprised to find him talking with a woman. But no one asked, "What do you want?" or "Why are you talking with her?"

²⁸Then, leaving her water jar, the woman went back to the town and said to the people, ²⁹"Come, see a man who told me everything I ever did. Could this be the Christ?" ³⁰They came out of the town and made their way toward him.

³¹Meanwhile his disciples urged him, "Rabbi, eat something."

³²But he said to them, "I have food to eat that you know nothing about."

³³Then his disciples said to each other, "Could someone have brought him food?"

³⁴"My food," said Jesus, "is to do the will of him who sent me and to finish his work. ³⁵Do you not say, 'Four months more and then the harvest'? I tell you, open your eyes and look at the fields! They are ripe for harvest. ³⁶Even now the reaper draws his wages, even now he harvests the crop for eternal life, so that the sower and the reaper may be glad together. ³⁷Thus the saying 'One sows and another reaps' is true. ³⁸I sent you to reap what

you have not worked for. Others have done the hard work, and you have reaped the benefits of their labor."

³⁹Many of the Samaritans from that town believed in him because of the woman's testimony, "He told me everything I ever did." ⁴⁰So when the Samaritans came to him, they urged him to stay with them, and he stayed two days. ⁴¹And because of his words many more became believers.

⁴²They said to the woman, "We no longer believe just because of what you said; now we have heard for ourselves, and we know that this man really is the Savior of the world."

⁴³After the two days he left for Galilee. ⁴⁴(Now Jesus himself had pointed out that a prophet has no honor in his own country.) ⁴⁵When he arrived in Galilee, the Galileans welcomed him. They had seen all that he had done in Jerusalem at the Passover Feast, for they also had been there.

⁴⁶Once more he visited Cana in Galilee, where he had turned the water into wine. And there was a certain royal official whose son lay sick at Capernaum. ⁴⁷When this man heard that Jesus had arrived in Galilee from Judea, he went to him and begged him to come and heal his son, who was close to death.

⁴⁸"Unless you people see miraculous signs and wonders," Jesus told him, "you will never believe."

⁴⁹The royal official said, "Sir, come down before my child dies."

⁵⁰Jesus replied, "You may go. Your son will live."

The man took Jesus at his word and departed. ⁵¹While he was still on the way, his servants met him with the news that his boy was living. ⁵²When he inquired as to the time when his son got better, they said to him, "The fever left him yesterday at the seventh hour."

⁵³Then the father realized that this was the exact time at which Jesus had said to him, "Your son will live." So he and all his household believed.

⁵⁴This was the second miraculous sign that Jesus performed, having come from Judea to Galilee.

5

Some time later, Jesus went up to Jerusalem for a feast of the Jews. ²Now there is in Jerusalem near the Sheep Gate a pool, which in Aramaic is called Bethesda and which is surrounded by five covered colonnades. ³Here a great number of disabled people used to lie—the blind, the lame, the paralyzed. ⁵One who was there had been an invalid for thirty-eight years. ⁶When Jesus saw him lying there and learned that he had been in this condition for a long time, he asked him, "Do you want to get well?"

⁷"Sir," the invalid replied, "I have no one to help me into the pool when the water is stirred. While I am trying to get in, someone else goes down ahead of me."

⁸Then Jesus said to him, "Get up! Pick up your mat and walk." ⁹At once the man was cured; he picked up his mat and walked.

The day on which this took place was a Sabbath, ¹⁰and so the Jews said to the man who had been healed, "It is the Sabbath; the law forbids you to carry your mat."

¹¹But he replied, "The man who made me well said to me, 'Pick up your mat and walk.'"

¹²So they asked him, "Who is this fellow who told you to pick it up and walk?"

¹³The man who was healed had no idea who it was, for Jesus had slipped away into the crowd that was there.

¹⁴Later Jesus found him at the temple and said to him, "See, you are well again. Stop sinning or something

worse may happen to you." [15]The man went away and told the Jews that it was Jesus who had made him well.

[16]So, because Jesus was doing these things on the Sabbath, the Jews persecuted him. [17]Jesus said to them, "My Father is always at his work to this very day, and I, too, am working." [18]For this reason the Jews tried all the harder to kill him; not only was he breaking the Sabbath, but he was even calling God his own Father, making himself equal with God.

[19]Jesus gave them this answer: "I tell you the truth, the Son can do nothing by himself; he can do only what he sees his Father doing, because whatever the Father does the Son also does. [20]For the Father loves the Son and shows him all he does. Yes, to your amazement he will show him even greater things than these. [21]For just as the Father raises the dead and gives them life, even so the Son gives life to whom he is pleased to give it. [22]Moreover, the Father judges no one, but has entrusted all judgment to the Son, [23]that all may honor the Son just as they honor the Father. He who does not honor the Son does not honor the Father, who sent him.

[24]"I tell you the truth, whoever hears my word and believes him who sent me has eternal life and will not be condemned; he has crossed over from death to life. [25]I tell you the truth, a time is coming and has now come when the dead will hear the voice of the Son of God and those who hear will live. [26]For as the Father has life in himself, so he has granted the Son to have life in himself. [27]And he has given him authority to judge because he is the Son of Man.

[28]"Do not be amazed at this, for a time is coming when all who are in their graves will hear his voice [29]and come out—those who have done good will rise to live, and those who have done evil will rise to be condemned. [30]By myself I can do nothing; I judge only as I hear, and

my judgment is just, for I seek not to please myself but him who sent me.

[31]"If I testify about myself, my testimony is not valid. [32]There is another who testifies in my favor, and I know that his testimony about me is valid.

[33]"You have sent to John and he has testified to the truth. [34]Not that I accept human testimony; but I mention it that you may be saved. [35]John was a lamp that burned and gave light, and you chose for a time to enjoy his light.

[36]"I have testimony weightier than that of John. For the very work that the Father has given me to finish, and which I am doing, testifies that the Father has sent me. [37]And the Father who sent me has himself testified concerning me. You have never heard his voice nor seen his form, [38]nor does his word dwell in you, for you do not believe the one he sent. [39]You diligently study the Scriptures because you think that by them you possess eternal life. These are the Scriptures that testify about me, [40]yet you refuse to come to me to have life.

[41]"I do not accept praise from men, [42]but I know you. I know that you do not have the love of God in your hearts. [43]I have come in my Father's name, and you do not accept me; but if someone else comes in his own name, you will accept him. [44]How can you believe if you accept praise from one another, yet make no effort to obtain the praise that comes from the only God?

[45]"But do not think I will accuse you before the Father. Your accuser is Moses, on whom your hopes are set. [46]If you believed Moses, you would believe me, for he wrote about me. [47]But since you do not believe what he wrote, how are you going to believe what I say?"

6

Some time after this, Jesus crossed to the far shore of the Sea of Galilee (that is, the Sea of Tiberias), ²and a great crowd of people followed him because they saw the miraculous signs he had performed on the sick. ³Then Jesus went up on a mountainside and sat down with his disciples. ⁴The Jewish Passover Feast was near.

⁵When Jesus looked up and saw a great crowd coming toward him, he said to Philip, "Where shall we buy bread for these people to eat?" ⁶He asked this only to test him, for he already had in mind what he was going to do.

⁷Philip answered him, "Eight months' wages would not buy enough bread for each one to have a bite!"

⁸Another of his disciples, Andrew, Simon Peter's brother, spoke up, ⁹"Here is a boy with five small barley loaves and two small fish, but how far will they go among so many?"

¹⁰Jesus said, "Have the people sit down." There was plenty of grass in that place, and the men sat down, about five thousand of them. ¹¹Jesus then took the loaves, gave thanks, and distributed to those who were seated as much as they wanted. He did the same with the fish.

¹²When they had all had enough to eat, he said to his disciples, "Gather the pieces that are left over. Let nothing be wasted." ¹³So they gathered them and filled twelve baskets with the pieces of the five barley loaves left over by those who had eaten.

¹⁴After the people saw the miraculous sign that Jesus did, they began to say, "Surely this is the Prophet who is to come into the world." ¹⁵Jesus, knowing that they intended to come and make him king by force, withdrew again to a mountain by himself.

[16]When evening came, his disciples went down to the lake, [17]where they got into a boat and set off across the lake for Capernaum. By now it was dark, and Jesus had not yet joined them. [18]A strong wind was blowing and the waters grew rough. [19]When they had rowed three or three and a half miles, they saw Jesus approaching the boat, walking on the water; and they were terrified. [20]But he said to them, "It is I; don't be afraid." [21]Then they were willing to take him into the boat, and immediately the boat reached the shore where they were heading.

[22]The next day the crowd that had stayed on the opposite shore of the lake realized that only one boat had been there, and that Jesus had not entered it with his disciples, but that they had gone away alone. [23]Then some boats from Tiberias landed near the place where the people had eaten the bread after the Lord had given thanks. [24]Once the crowd realized that neither Jesus nor his disciples were there, they got into the boats and went to Capernaum in search of Jesus.

[25]When they found him on the other side of the lake, they asked him, "Rabbi, when did you get here?"

[26]Jesus answered, "I tell you the truth, you are looking for me, not because you saw miraculous signs but because you ate the loaves and had your fill. [27]Do not work for food that spoils, but for food that endures to eternal life, which the Son of Man will give you. On him God the Father has placed his seal of approval."

[28]Then they asked him, "What must we do to do the works God requires?"

[29]Jesus answered, "The work of God is this: to believe in the one he has sent."

[30]So they asked him, "What miraculous sign then will you give that we may see it and believe you? What will you do? [31]Our forefathers ate the manna in the desert; as it is written: 'He gave them bread from heaven to eat.'"

³²Jesus said to them, "I tell you the truth, it is not Moses who has given you the bread from heaven, but it is my Father who gives you the true bread from heaven. ³³For the bread of God is he who comes down from heaven and gives life to the world."

³⁴"Sir," they said, "from now on give us this bread."

³⁵Then Jesus declared, "I am the bread of life. He who comes to me will never go hungry, and he who believes in me will never be thirsty. ³⁶But as I told you, you have seen me and still you do not believe. ³⁷All that the Father gives me will come to me, and whoever comes to me I will never drive away. ³⁸For I have come down from heaven not to do my will but to do the will of him who sent me. ³⁹And this is the will of him who sent me, that I shall lose none of all that he has given me, but raise them up at the last day. ⁴⁰For my Father's will is that everyone who looks to the Son and believes in him shall have eternal life, and I will raise him up at the last day."

⁴¹At this the Jews began to grumble about him because he said, "I am the bread that came down from heaven." ⁴²They said, "Is this not Jesus, the son of Joseph, whose father and mother we know? How can he now say, 'I came down from heaven'?"

⁴³"Stop grumbling among yourselves," Jesus answered. ⁴⁴"No one can come to me unless the Father who sent me draws him, and I will raise him up at the last day. ⁴⁵It is written in the Prophets: 'They will all be taught by God.' Everyone who listens to the Father and learns from him comes to me. ⁴⁶No one has seen the Father except the one who is from God; only he has seen the Father. ⁴⁷I tell you the truth, he who believes has everlasting life. ⁴⁸I am the bread of life. ⁴⁹Your forefathers ate the manna in the desert, yet they died. ⁵⁰But here is the bread that comes down from heaven, which a man may eat and not die. ⁵¹I am the living bread that

came down from heaven. If anyone eats of this bread, he will live forever. This bread is my flesh, which I will give for the life of the world."

[52] Then the Jews began to argue sharply among themselves, "How can this man give us his flesh to eat?"

[53] Jesus said to them, "I tell you the truth, unless you eat the flesh of the Son of Man and drink his blood, you have no life in you. [54] Whoever eats my flesh and drinks my blood has eternal life, and I will raise him up at the last day. [55] For my flesh is real food and my blood is real drink. [56] Whoever eats my flesh and drinks my blood remains in me, and I in him. [57] Just as the living Father sent me and I live because of the Father, so the one who feeds on me will live because of me. [58] This is the bread that came down from heaven. Your forefathers ate manna and died, but he who feeds on this bread will live forever." [59] He said this while teaching in the synagogue in Capernaum.

[60] On hearing it, many of his disciples said, "This is a hard teaching. Who can accept it?"

[61] Aware that his disciples were grumbling about this, Jesus said to them, "Does this offend you? [62] What if you see the Son of Man ascend to where he was before! [63] The Spirit gives life; the flesh counts for nothing. The words I have spoken to you are spirit and they are life. [64] Yet there are some of you who do not believe." For Jesus had known from the beginning which of them did not believe and who would betray him. [65] He went on to say, "This is why I told you that no one can come to me unless the Father has enabled him."

[66] From this time many of his disciples turned back and no longer followed him.

[67] "You do not want to leave too, do you?" Jesus asked the Twelve.

⁶⁸Simon Peter answered him, "Lord, to whom shall we go? You have the words of eternal life. ⁶⁹We believe and know that you are the Holy One of God."

⁷⁰Then Jesus replied, "Have I not chosen you, the Twelve? Yet one of you is a devil!" ⁷¹(He meant Judas, the son of Simon Iscariot, who, though one of the Twelve, was later to betray him.)

7

After this, Jesus went around in Galilee, purposely staying away from Judea because the Jews there were waiting to take his life. ²But when the Jewish Feast of Tabernacles was near, ³Jesus' brothers said to him, "You ought to leave here and go to Judea, so that your disciples may see the miracles you do. ⁴No one who wants to become a public figure acts in secret. Since you are doing these things, show yourself to the world." ⁵For even his own brothers did not believe in him.

⁶Therefore Jesus told them, "The right time for me has not yet come; for you any time is right. ⁷The world cannot hate you, but it hates me because I testify that what it does is evil. ⁸You go to the Feast. I am not yet going up to this Feast, because for me the right time has not yet come." ⁹Having said this, he stayed in Galilee.

¹⁰However, after his brothers had left for the Feast, he went also, not publicly, but in secret. ¹¹Now at the Feast the Jews were watching for him and asking, "Where is that man?"

¹²Among the crowds there was wide-spread whispering about him. Some said, "He is a good man."

Others replied, "No, he deceives the people." ¹³But no one would say anything publicly about him for fear of the Jews.

¹⁴Not until halfway through the Feast did Jesus go up to the temple courts and begin to teach. ¹⁵The Jews were

amazed and asked, "How did this man get such learning without having studied?"

[16]Jesus answered, "My teaching is not my own. It comes from him who sent me. [17]If anyone chooses to do God's will, he will find out whether my teaching comes from God or whether I speak on my own. [18]He who speaks on his own does so to gain honor for himself, but he who works for the honor of the one who sent him is a man of truth; there is nothing false about him. [19]Has not Moses given you the law? Yet not one of you keeps the law. Why are you trying to kill me?"

[20]"You are demon-possessed," the crowd answered. "Who is trying to kill you?"

[21]Jesus said to them, "I did one miracle, and you are all astonished. [22]Yet, because Moses gave you circumcision (though actually it did not come from Moses, but from the patriarchs), you circumcise a child on the Sabbath. [23]Now if a child can be circumcised on the Sabbath so that the law of Moses may not be broken, why are you angry with me for healing the whole man on the Sabbath? [24]Stop judging by mere appearances, and make a right judgment."

[25]At that point some of the people of Jerusalem began to ask, "Isn't this the man they are trying to kill? [26]Here he is, speaking publicly, and they are not saying a word to him. Have the authorities really concluded that he is the Christ? [27]But we know where this man is from; when the Christ comes, no one will know where he is from."

[28]Then Jesus, still teaching in the temple courts, cried out, "Yes, you know me, and you know where I am from. I am not here on my own, but he who sent me is true. You do not know him, [29]but I know him because I am from him and he sent me."

³⁰At this they tried to seize him, but no one laid a hand on him, because his time had not yet come. ³¹Still, many in the crowd put their faith in him. They said, "When the Christ comes, will he do more miraculous signs than this man?"

³²The Pharisees heard the crowd whispering such things about him. Then the chief priests and the Pharisees sent temple guards to arrest him.

³³Jesus said, "I am with you for only a short time, and then I go to the one who sent me. ³⁴You will look for me, but you will not find me; and where I am, you cannot come."

³⁵The Jews said to one another, "Where does this man intend to go that we cannot find him? Will he go where our people live scattered among the Greeks, and teach the Greeks? ³⁶What did he mean when he said, 'You will look for me, but you will not find me,' and 'Where I am, you cannot come'?"

³⁷On the last and greatest day of the Feast, Jesus stood and said in a loud voice, "If anyone is thirsty, let him come to me and drink. ³⁸Whoever believes in me, as the Scripture has said, streams of living water will flow from within him." ³⁹By this he meant the Spirit, whom those who believed in him were later to receive. Up to that time the Spirit had not been given, since Jesus had not yet been glorified.

⁴⁰On hearing his words, some of the people said, "Surely this man is the Prophet."

⁴¹Others said, "He is the Christ."

Still others asked, "How can the Christ come from Galilee? ⁴²Does not the Scripture say that the Christ will come from David's family and from Bethlehem, the town where David lived?" ⁴³Thus the people were divided because of Jesus. ⁴⁴Some wanted to seize him, but no one laid a hand on him.

⁴⁵Finally the temple guards went back to the chief priests and Pharisees, who asked them, "Why didn't you bring him in?"

⁴⁶"No one ever spoke the way this man does," the guards declared.

⁴⁷"You mean he has deceived you also?" the Pharisees retorted. ⁴⁸"Has any of the rulers or of the Pharisees believed in him? ⁴⁹No! But this mob that knows nothing of the law—there is a curse on them."

⁵⁰Nicodemus, who had gone to Jesus earlier and who was one of their own number, asked, ⁵¹"Does our law condemn anyone without first hearing him to find out what he is doing?"

⁵²They replied, "Are you from Galilee, too? Look into it, and you will find that a prophet does not come out of Galilee."

⁵³Then each went to his own home.

8

But Jesus went to the Mount of Olives. ²At dawn he appeared again in the temple courts, where all the people gathered around him, and he sat down to teach them. ³The teachers of the law and the Pharisees brought in a woman caught in adultery. They made her stand before the group ⁴and said to Jesus, "Teacher, this woman was caught in the act of adultery. ⁵In the Law Moses commanded us to stone such women. Now what do you say?" ⁶They were using this question as a trap, in order to have a basis for accusing him.

But Jesus bent down and started to write on the ground with his finger. ⁷When they kept on questioning him, he straightened up and said to them, "If any one of you is without sin, let him be the first to throw a stone at her." ⁸Again he stooped down and wrote on the ground.

⁹At this, those who heard began to go away one at a time, the older ones first, until only Jesus was left, with the woman still standing there. ¹⁰Jesus straightened up and asked her, "Woman, where are they? Has no one condemned you?"

¹¹"No one, sir," she said.

"Then neither do I condemn you," Jesus declared. "Go now and leave your life of sin."

¹²When Jesus spoke again to the people, he said, "I am the light of the world. Whoever follows me will never walk in darkness, but will have the light of life."

¹³The Pharisees challenged him, "Here you are, appearing as your own witness; your testimony is not valid."

¹⁴Jesus answered, "Even if I testify on my own behalf, my testimony is valid, for I know where I came from and where I am going. But you have no idea where I come from or where I am going. ¹⁵You judge by human standards; I pass judgment on no one. ¹⁶But if I do judge, my decisions are right, because I am not alone. I stand with the Father, who sent me. ¹⁷In your own Law it is written that the testimony of two men is valid. ¹⁸I am one who testifies for myself; my other witness is the Father, who sent me."

¹⁹Then they asked him, "Where is your father?"

"You do not know me or my Father," Jesus replied. "If you knew me, you would know my Father also." ²⁰He spoke these words while teaching in the temple area near the place where the offerings were put. Yet no one seized him, because his time had not yet come.

²¹Once more Jesus said to them, "I am going away, and you will look for me, and you will die in your sin. Where I go, you cannot come."

²²This made the Jews ask, "Will he kill himself? Is that why he says, 'Where I go, you cannot come'?"

[23] But he continued, "You are from below; I am from above. You are of this world; I am not of this world. [24] I told you that you would die in your sins; if you do not believe that I am [the one I claim to be], you will indeed die in your sins."

[25] "Who are you?" they asked.

"Just what I have been claiming all along," Jesus replied. [26] "I have much to say in judgment of you. But he who sent me is reliable, and what I have heard from him I tell the world."

[27] They did not understand that he was telling them about his Father. [28] So Jesus said, "When you have lifted up the Son of Man, then you will know that I am [the one I claim to be] and that I do nothing on my own but speak just what the Father has taught me. [29] The one who sent me is with me; he has not left me alone, for I always do what pleases him." [30] Even as he spoke, many put their faith in him.

[31] To the Jews who had believed him, Jesus said, "If you hold to my teaching, you are really my disciples. [32] Then you will know the truth, and the truth will set you free."

[33] They answered him, "We are Abraham's descendants and have never been slaves of anyone. How can you say that we shall be set free?"

[34] Jesus replied, "I tell you the truth, everyone who sins is a slave to sin. [35] Now a slave has no permanent place in the family, but a son belongs to it forever. [36] So if the Son sets you free, you will be free indeed. [37] I know you are Abraham's descendants. Yet you are ready to kill me, because you have no room for my word. [38] I am telling you what I have seen in the Father's presence, and you do what you have heard from your father."

[39] "Abraham is our father," they answered.

"If you were Abraham's children," said Jesus, "then you would do the things Abraham did. [40]As it is, you are determined to kill me, a man who has told you the truth that I heard from God. Abraham did not do such things. [41]You are doing the things your own father does."

"We are not illegitimate children," they protested. "The only Father we have is God himself."

[42]Jesus said to them, "If God were your Father, you would love me, for I came from God and now am here. I have not come on my own; but he sent me. [43]Why is my language not clear to you? Because you are unable to hear what I say. [44]You belong to your father, the devil, and you want to carry out your father's desire. He was a murderer from the beginning, not holding to the truth, for there is no truth in him. When he lies, he speaks his native language, for he is a liar and the father of lies. [45]Yet because I tell the truth, you do not believe me! [46]Can any of you prove me guilty of sin? If I am telling the truth, why don't you believe me? [47]He who belongs to God hears what God says. The reason you do not hear is that you do not belong to God."

[48]The Jews answered him, "Aren't we right in saying that you are a Samaritan and demon-possessed?"

[49]"I am not possessed by a demon," said Jesus, "but I honor my Father and you dishonor me. [50]I am not seeking glory for myself; but there is one who seeks it, and he is the judge. [51]I tell you the truth, if anyone keeps my word, he will never see death."

[52]At this the Jews exclaimed, "Now we know that you are demon-possessed! Abraham died and so did the prophets, yet you say that if anyone keeps your word, he will never taste death. [53]Are you greater than our father Abraham? He died, and so did the prophets. Who do you think you are?"

⁵⁴Jesus replied, "If I glorify myself, my glory means nothing. My Father, whom you claim as your God, is the one who glorifies me. ⁵⁵Though you do not know him, I know him. If I said I did not, I would be a liar like you, but I do know him and keep his word. ⁵⁶Your father Abraham rejoiced at the thought of seeing my day; he saw it and was glad."

⁵⁷"You are not yet fifty years old," the Jews said to him, "and you have seen Abraham!"

⁵⁸"I tell you the truth," Jesus answered, "before Abraham was born, I am!" ⁵⁹At this, they picked up stones to stone him, but Jesus hid himself, slipping away from the temple grounds.

9

As he went along, he saw a man blind from birth. ²His disciples asked him, "Rabbi, who sinned, this man or his parents, that he was born blind?"

³"Neither this man nor his parents sinned," said Jesus, "but this happened so that the work of God might be displayed in his life. ⁴As long as it is day, we must do the work of him who sent me. Night is coming, when no one can work. ⁵While I am in the world, I am the light of the world."

⁶Having said this, he spit on the ground, made some mud with the saliva, and put it on the man's eyes. ⁷"Go," he told him, "wash in the Pool of Siloam" (this word means Sent). So the man went and washed, and came home seeing.

⁸His neighbors and those who had formerly seen him begging asked, "Isn't this the same man who used to sit and beg?" ⁹Some claimed that he was.

Others said, "No, he only looks like him."

But he himself insisted, "I am the man."

[10]"How then were your eyes opened?" they demanded.

[11]He replied, "The man they call Jesus made some mud and put it on my eyes. He told me to go to Siloam and wash. So I went and washed, and then I could see."

[12]"Where is this man?" they asked him.

"I don't know," he said.

[13]They brought to the Pharisees the man who had been blind. [14]Now the day on which Jesus had made the mud and opened the man's eyes was a Sabbath. [15]Therefore the Pharisees also asked him how he had received his sight. "He put mud on my eyes," the man replied, "and I washed, and now I see."

[16]Some of the Pharisees said, "This man is not from God, for he does not keep the Sabbath."

But others asked, "How can a sinner do such miraculous signs?" So they were divided.

[17]Finally they turned again to the blind man, "What have you to say about him? It was your eyes he opened."

The man replied, "He is a prophet."

[18]The Jews still did not believe that he had been blind and had received his sight until they sent for the man's parents. [19]"Is this your son?" they asked. "Is this the one you say was born blind? How is it that now he can see?"

[20]"We know he is our son," the parents answered, "and we know he was born blind. [21]But how he can see now, or who opened his eyes, we don't know. Ask him. He is of age; he will speak for himself." [22]His parents said this because they were afraid of the Jews, for already the Jews had decided that anyone who acknowledged that Jesus was the Christ would be put out of the synagogue. [23]That was why his parents said, "He is of age; ask him."

[24]A second time they summoned the man who had been blind. "Give glory to God," they said. "We know this man is a sinner."

^{25}He replied, "Whether he is a sinner or not, I don't know. One thing I do know. I was blind but now I see!"

^{26}Then they asked him, "What did he do to you? How did he open your eyes?"

^{27}He answered, "I have told you already and you did not listen. Why do you want to hear it again? Do you want to become his disciples, too?"

^{28}Then they hurled insults at him and said, "You are this fellow's disciple! We are disciples of Moses! ^{29}We know that God spoke to Moses, but as for this fellow, we don't even know where he comes from."

^{30}The man answered, "Now that is remarkable! You don't know where he comes from, yet he opened my eyes. ^{31}We know that God does not listen to sinners. He listens to the godly man who does his will. ^{32}Nobody has ever heard of opening the eyes of a man born blind. ^{33}If this man were not from God, he could do nothing."

^{34}To this they replied, "You were steeped in sin at birth; how dare you lecture us!" And they threw him out.

^{35}Jesus heard that they had thrown him out, and when he found him, he said, "Do you believe in the Son of Man?"

^{36}"Who is he, sir?" the man asked. "Tell me so that I may believe in him."

^{37}Jesus said, "You have now seen him; in fact, he is the one speaking with you."

^{38}Then the man said, "Lord, I believe," and he worshiped him.

^{39}Jesus said, "For judgment I have come into this world, so that the blind will see and those who see will become blind."

^{40}Some Pharisees who were with him heard him say this and asked, "What? Are we blind too?"

⁴¹Jesus said, "If you were blind, you would not be guilty of sin; but now that you claim you can see, your guilt remains.

10

"I tell you the truth, the man who does not enter the sheep pen by the gate, but climbs in by some other way, is a thief and a robber. ²The man who enters by the gate is the shepherd of his sheep. ³The watchman opens the gate for him, and the sheep listen to his voice. He calls his own sheep by name and leads them out. ⁴When he has brought out all his own, he goes on ahead of them, and his sheep follow him because they know his voice. ⁵But they will never follow a stranger; in fact, they will run away from him because they do not recognize a stranger's voice." ⁶Jesus used this figure of speech, but they did not understand what he was telling them.

⁷Therefore Jesus said again, "I tell you the truth, I am the gate for the sheep. ⁸All who ever came before me were thieves and robbers, but the sheep did not listen to them. ⁹I am the gate; whoever enters through me will be saved. He will come in and go out, and find pasture. ¹⁰The thief comes only to steal and kill and destroy; I have come that they may have life, and have it to the full.

¹¹"I am the good shepherd. The good shepherd lays down his life for the sheep. ¹²The hired hand is not the shepherd who owns the sheep. So when he sees the wolf coming, he abandons the sheep and runs away. Then the wolf attacks the flock and scatters it. ¹³The man runs away because he is a hired hand and cares nothing for the sheep.

¹⁴"I am the good shepherd; I know my sheep and my sheep know me—¹⁵just as the Father knows me and I know the Father—and I lay down my life for the sheep.

¹⁶I have other sheep that are not of this sheep pen. I must bring them also. They too will listen to my voice, and there shall be one flock and one shepherd. ¹⁷The reason my Father loves me is that I lay down my life— only to take it up again. ¹⁸No one takes it from me, but I lay it down of my own accord. I have authority to lay it down and authority to take it up again. This command I received from my Father."

¹⁹At these words the Jews were again divided. ²⁰Many of them said, "He is demon-possessed and raving mad. Why listen to him?"

²¹But others said, "These are not the sayings of a man possessed by a demon. Can a demon open the eyes of the blind?"

²²Then came the Feast of Dedication at Jerusalem. It was winter, ²³and Jesus was in the temple area walking in Solomon's Colonnade. ²⁴The Jews gathered around him, saying, "How long will you keep us in suspense? If you are the Christ, tell us plainly."

²⁵Jesus answered, "I did tell you, but you do not believe. The miracles I do in my Father's name speak for me, ²⁶but you do not believe because you are not my sheep. ²⁷My sheep listen to my voice; I know them, and they follow me. ²⁸I give them eternal life, and they shall never perish; no one can snatch them out of my hand. ²⁹My Father, who has given them to me, is greater than all; no one can snatch them out of my Father's hand. ³⁰I and the Father are one."

³¹Again the Jews picked up stones to stone him, ³²but Jesus said to them, "I have shown you many great miracles from the Father. For which of these do you stone me?"

³³"We are not stoning you for any of these," replied the Jews, "but for blasphemy, because you, a mere man, claim to be God."

³⁴Jesus answered them, "Is it not written in your Law, 'I have said you are gods'? ³⁵If he called them 'gods,' to whom the word of God came—and the Scripture cannot be broken—³⁶what about the one whom the Father set apart as his very own and sent into the world? Why then do you accuse me of blasphemy because I said, 'I am God's Son'? ³⁷Do not believe me unless I do what my Father does. ³⁸But if I do it, even though you do not believe me, believe the miracles, that you may know and understand that the Father is in me, and I in the Father." ³⁹Again they tried to seize him, but he escaped their grasp.

⁴⁰Then Jesus went back across the Jordan to the place where John had been baptizing in the early days. Here he stayed ⁴¹and many people came to him. They said, "Though John never performed a miraculous sign, all that John said about this man was true." ⁴²And in that place many believed in Jesus.

11

Now a man named Lazarus was sick. He was from Bethany, the village of Mary and her sister Martha. ²This Mary, whose brother Lazarus now lay sick, was the same one who poured perfume on the Lord and wiped his feet with her hair. ³So the sisters sent word to Jesus, "Lord, the one you love is sick."

⁴When he heard this, Jesus said, "This sickness will not end in death. No, it is for God's glory so that God's Son may be glorified through it." ⁵Jesus loved Martha and her sister and Lazarus. ⁶Yet when he heard that Lazarus was sick, he stayed where he was two more days.

⁷Then he said to his disciples, "Let us go back to Judea."

⁸"But Rabbi," they said, "a short while ago the Jews tried to stone you, and yet you are going back there?"

[9]Jesus answered, "Are there not twelve hours of daylight? A man who walks by day will not stumble, for he sees by this world's light. [10]It is when he walks by night that he stumbles, for he has no light."

[11]After he had said this, he went on to tell them, "Our friend Lazarus has fallen asleep; but I am going there to wake him up."

[12]His disciples replied, "Lord, if he sleeps, he will get better." [13]Jesus had been speaking of his death, but his disciples thought he meant natural sleep.

[14]So then he told them plainly, "Lazarus is dead, [15]and for your sake I am glad I was not there, so that you may believe. But let us go to him."

[16]Then Thomas (called Didymus) said to the rest of the disciples, "Let us also go, that we may die with him."

[17]On his arrival, Jesus found that Lazarus had already been in the tomb for four days. [18]Bethany was less than two miles from Jerusalem, [19]and many Jews had come to Martha and Mary to comfort them in the loss of their brother. [20]When Martha heard that Jesus was coming, she went out to meet him, but Mary stayed at home.

[21]"Lord," Martha said to Jesus, "if you had been here, my brother would not have died. [22]But I know that even now God will give you whatever you ask."

[23]Jesus said to her, "Your brother will rise again."

[24]Martha answered, "I know he will rise again in the resurrection at the last day."

[25]Jesus said to her, "I am the resurrection and the life. He who believes in me will live, even though he dies; [26]and whoever lives and believes in me will never die. Do you believe this?"

[27]"Yes, Lord," she told him, "I believe that you are the Christ, the Son of God, who was to come into the world."

²⁸And after she had said this, she went back and called her sister Mary aside. "The Teacher is here," she said, "and is asking for you." ²⁹When Mary heard this, she got up quickly and went to him. ³⁰Now Jesus had not yet entered the village, but was still at the place where Martha had met him. ³¹When the Jews who had been with Mary in the house, comforting her, noticed how quickly she got up and went out, they followed her, supposing she was going to the tomb to mourn there.

³²When Mary reached the place where Jesus was and saw him, she fell at his feet and said, "Lord, if you had been here, my brother would not have died."

³³When Jesus saw her weeping, and the Jews who had come along with her also weeping, he was deeply moved in spirit and troubled. ³⁴"Where have you laid him?" he asked.

"Come and see, Lord," they replied.

³⁵Jesus wept.

³⁶Then the Jews said, "See how he loved him!"

³⁷But some of them said, "Could not he who opened the eyes of the blind man have kept this man from dying?"

³⁸Jesus, once more deeply moved, came to the tomb. It was a cave with a stone laid across the entrance. ³⁹"Take away the stone," he said.

"But, Lord," said Martha, the sister of the dead man, "by this time there is a bad odor, for he has been there four days."

⁴⁰Then Jesus said, "Did I not tell you that if you believed, you would see the glory of God?"

⁴¹So they took away the stone. Then Jesus looked up and said, "Father, I thank you that you have heard me. ⁴²I knew that you always hear me, but I said this for the benefit of the people standing here, that they may believe that you sent me."

^{43}When he had said this, Jesus called in a loud voice, "Lazarus, come out!" ^{44}The dead man came out, his hands and feet wrapped with strips of linen, and a cloth around his face.

Jesus said to them, "Take off the grave clothes and let him go."

^{45}Therefore many of the Jews who had come to visit Mary, and had seen what Jesus did, put their faith in him. ^{46}But some of them went to the Pharisees and told them what Jesus had done. ^{47}Then the chief priests and the Pharisees called a meeting of the Sanhedrin.

"What are we accomplishing?" they asked. "Here is this man performing many miraculous signs. ^{48}If we let him go on like this, everyone will believe in him, and then the Romans will come and take away both our place and our nation."

^{49}Then one of them, named Caiaphas, who was high priest that year, spoke up, "You know nothing at all! ^{50}You do not realize that it is better for you that one man die for the people than that the whole nation perish."

^{51}He did not say this on his own, but as high priest that year he prophesied that Jesus would die for the Jewish nation, ^{52}and not only for that nation but also for the scattered children of God, to bring them together and make them one. ^{53}So from that day on they plotted to take his life.

^{54}Therefore Jesus no longer moved about publicly among the Jews. Instead he withdrew to a region near the desert, to a village called Ephraim, where he stayed with his disciples.

^{55}When it was almost time for the Jewish Passover, many went up from the country to Jerusalem for their ceremonial cleansing before the Passover. ^{56}They kept looking for Jesus, and as they stood in the temple area they asked one another, "What do you think? Isn't he coming to the Feast at all?" ⁵⁷But the chief priests and Pharisees had given orders that if anyone found out where Jesus was, he should report it so that they might arrest him.

12

Six days before the Passover, Jesus arrived at Bethany, where Lazarus lived, whom Jesus had raised from the dead. ²Here a dinner was given in Jesus' honor. Martha served, while Lazarus was among those reclining at the table with him. ³Then Mary took about a pint of pure nard, an expensive perfume; she poured it on Jesus' feet and wiped his feet with her hair. And the house was filled with the fragrance of the perfume.

⁴But one of his disciples, Judas Iscariot, who was later to betray him, objected, ⁵"Why wasn't this perfume sold and the money given to the poor? It was worth a year's wages." ⁶He did not say this because he cared about the poor but because he was a thief; as keeper of the money bag, he used to help himself to what was put into it.

⁷"Leave her alone," Jesus replied. "[It was intended] that she should save this perfume for the day of my burial. ⁸You will always have the poor among you, but you will not always have me."

⁹Meanwhile a large crowd of Jews found out that Jesus was there and came, not only because of him but also to see Lazarus, whom he had raised from the dead. ¹⁰So the chief priests made plans to kill Lazarus as well, ¹¹for on account of him many of the Jews were going over to Jesus and putting their faith in him.

¹²The next day the great crowd that had come for the Feast heard that Jesus was on his way to Jerusalem. ¹³They took palm branches and went out to meet him, shouting,

"Hosanna!"

"Blessed is he who comes in the name of the Lord!"

"Blessed is the King of Israel!"

[14]Jesus found a young donkey and sat upon it, as it is written,

> [15]"Do not be afraid, O Daughter of Zion;
> see, your king is coming,
> seated on a donkey's colt."

[16]At first his disciples did not understand all this. Only after Jesus was glorified did they realize that these things had been written about him and that they had done these things to him.

[17]Now the crowd that was with him when he called Lazarus from the tomb and raised him from the dead continued to spread the word. [18]Many people, because they had heard that he had given this miraculous sign, went out to meet him. [19]So the Pharisees said to one another, "See, this is getting us nowhere. Look how the whole world has gone after him!"

[20]Now there were some Greeks among those who went up to worship at the Feast. [21]They came to Philip, who was from Bethsaida in Galilee, with a request. "Sir," they said, "we would like to see Jesus." [22]Philip went to tell Andrew; Andrew and Philip in turn told Jesus.

[23]Jesus replied, "The hour has come for the Son of Man to be glorified. [24]I tell you the truth, unless a kernel of wheat falls to the ground and dies, it remains only a single seed. But if it dies, it produces many seeds. [25]The man who loves his life will lose it, while the man who hates his life in this world will keep it for eternal life. [26]Whoever serves me must follow me; and where I am,

my servant also will be. My Father will honor the one who serves me.

[27]"Now my heart is troubled, and what shall I say? 'Father, save me from this hour'? No, it was for this very reason I came to this hour. [28]Father, glorify your name!"

Then a voice came from heaven, "I have glorified it, and will glorify it again." [29]The crowd that was there and heard it said it had thundered; others said an angel had spoken to him.

[30]Jesus said, "This voice was for your benefit, not mine. [31]Now is the time for judgment on this world; now the prince of this world will be driven out. [32]But I, when I am lifted up from the earth, will draw all men to myself." [33]He said this to show the kind of death he was going to die.

[34]The crowd spoke up, "We have heard from the Law that the Christ will remain forever, so how can you say, 'The Son of Man must be lifted up'? Who is this 'Son of Man'?"

[35]Then Jesus told them, "You are going to have the light just a little while longer. Walk while you have the light, before darkness overtakes you. The man who walks in the dark does not know where he is going. [36]Put your trust in the light while you have it, so that you may become sons of light." When he had finished speaking, Jesus left and hid himself from them.

[37]Even after Jesus had done all these miraculous signs in their presence, they still would not believe in him. [38]This was to fulfill the word of Isaiah the prophet:

"Lord, who has believed our message
and to whom has the arm of the Lord been
revealed?"

[39]For this reason they could not believe, because, as Isaiah says elsewhere:

[40]"He has blinded their eyes
and deadened their hearts,
so they can neither see with their eyes,
nor understand with their hearts,
nor turn—and I would heal them."

[41]Isaiah said this because he saw Jesus' glory and spoke about him.

[42]Yet at the same time many even among the leaders believed in him. But because of the Pharisees they would not confess their faith for fear they would be put out of the synagogue; [43]for they loved praise from men more than praise from God.

[44]Then Jesus cried out, "When a man believes in me, he does not believe in me only, but in the one who sent me. [45]When he looks at me, he sees the one who sent me. [46]I have come into the world as a light, so that no one who believes in me should stay in darkness.

[47]"As for the person who hears my words but does not keep them, I do not judge him. For I did not come to judge the world, but to save it. [48]There is a judge for the one who rejects me and does not accept my words; that very word which I spoke will condemn him at the last day. [49]For I did not speak of my own accord, but the Father who sent me commanded me what to say and how to say it. [50]I know that his command leads to eternal life. So whatever I say is just what the Father has told me to say."

13

It was just before the Passover Feast. Jesus knew that the time had come for him to leave this world and go to the Father. Having loved his own who were in the world, he now showed them the full extent of his love.

²The evening meal was being served, and the devil had already prompted Judas Iscariot, son of Simon, to betray Jesus. ³Jesus knew that the Father had put all things under his power, and that he had come from God and was returning to God; ⁴so he got up from the meal, took off his outer clothing, and wrapped a towel around his waist. ⁵After that, he poured water into a basin and began to wash his disciples' feet, drying them with the towel that was wrapped around him.

⁶He came to Simon Peter, who said to him, "Lord, are you going to wash my feet?"

⁷Jesus replied, "You do not realize now what I am doing, but later you will understand."

⁸"No," said Peter, "you shall never wash my feet."

Jesus answered, "Unless I wash you, you have no part with me."

⁹"Then, Lord," Simon Peter replied, "not just my feet but my hands and my head as well!"

¹⁰Jesus answered, "A person who has had a bath needs only to wash his feet; his whole body is clean. And you are clean, though not every one of you." ¹¹For he knew who was going to betray him, and that was why he said not every one was clean.

¹²When he had finished washing their feet, he put on his clothes and returned to his place. "Do you understand what I have done for you?" he asked them. ¹³"You call me 'Teacher' and 'Lord,' and rightly so, for that is what I am. ¹⁴Now that I, your Lord and Teacher, have washed your feet, you also should wash one another's feet. ¹⁵I have set you an example that you should do as I have done for you. ¹⁶I tell you the truth, no servant is greater than his master, nor is a messenger greater than the one

who sent him. [17]Now that you know these things, you will be blessed if you do them.

[18]"I am not referring to all of you; I know those I have chosen. But this is to fulfill the scripture: 'He who shares my bread has lifted up his heel against me.'

[19]"I am telling you now before it happens, so that when it does happen you will believe that I am He. [20]I tell you the truth, whoever accepts anyone I send accepts me; and whoever accepts me accepts the one who sent me."

[21]After he had said this, Jesus was troubled in spirit and testified, "I tell you the truth, one of you is going to betray me."

[22]His disciples stared at one another, at a loss to know which of them he meant. [23]One of them, the disciple whom Jesus loved, was reclining next to him. [24]Simon Peter motioned to this disciple and said, "Ask him which one he means."

[25]Leaning back against Jesus, he asked him, "Lord, who is it?"

[26]Jesus answered, "It is the one to whom I will give this piece of bread when I have dipped it in the dish." Then, dipping the piece of bread, he gave it to Judas Iscariot, son of Simon. [27]As soon as Judas took the bread, Satan entered into him.

"What you are about to do, do quickly," Jesus told him, [28]but no one at the meal understood why Jesus said this to him. [29]Since Judas had charge of the money, some thought Jesus was telling him to buy what was needed for the Feast, or to give something to the poor. [30]As soon as Judas had taken the bread, he went out. And it was night.

[31]When he was gone, Jesus said, "Now is the Son of Man glorified and God is glorified in him. [32]If God is

glorified in him, God will glorify the Son in himself, and will glorify him at once.

[33]"My children, I will be with you only a little longer. You will look for me, and just as I told the Jews, so I tell you now: Where I am going, you cannot come.

[34]"A new command I give you: Love one another. As I have loved you, so you must love one another. [35]By this all men will know that you are my disciples, if you love one another."

[36]Simon Peter asked him, "Lord, where are you going?"

Jesus replied, "Where I am going, you cannot follow now, but you will follow later."

[37]Peter asked, "Lord, why can't I follow you now? I will lay down my life for you."

[38]Then Jesus answered, "Will you really lay down your life for me? I tell you the truth, before the rooster crows, you will disown me three times!

14

"Do not let your hearts be troubled. Trust in God; trust also in me. [2]In my Father's house are many rooms; if it were not so, I would have told you. I am going there to prepare a place for you. [3]And if I go and prepare a place for you, I will come back and take you to be with me that you also may be where I am. [4]You know the way to the place where I am going."

[5]Thomas said to him, "Lord, we don't know where you are going, so how can we know the way?"

[6]Jesus answered, "I am the way and the truth and the life. No one comes to the Father except through me. [7]If you really knew me, you would know my Father as well. From now on, you do know him and have seen him."

[8]Philip said, "Lord, show us the Father and that will be enough for us."

⁹Jesus answered: "Don't you know me, Philip, even after I have been among you such a long time? Anyone who has seen me has seen the Father. How can you say, 'Show us the Father'? ¹⁰Don't you believe that I am in the Father, and that the Father is in me? The words I say to you are not just my own. Rather, it is the Father, living in me, who is doing his work. ¹¹Believe me when I say that I am in the Father and the Father is in me; or at least believe on the evidence of the miracles themselves. ¹²I tell you the truth, anyone who has faith in me will do what I have been doing. He will do even greater things than these, because I am going to the Father. ¹³And I will do whatever you ask in my name, so that the Son may bring glory to the Father. ¹⁴You may ask me for anything in my name, and I will do it.

¹⁵"If you love me, you will obey what I command. ¹⁶And I will ask the Father, and he will give you another Counselor to be with you forever— ¹⁷the Spirit of truth. The world cannot accept him, because it neither sees him nor knows him. But you know him, for he lives with you and will be in you. ¹⁸I will not leave you as orphans; I will come to you. ¹⁹Before long, the world will not see me anymore, but you will see me. Because I live, you also will live. ²⁰On that day you will realize that I am in my Father, and you are in me, and I am in you. ²¹Whoever has my commands and obeys them, he is the one who loves me. He who loves me will be loved by my Father, and I too will love him and show myself to him."

²²Then Judas (not Judas Iscariot) said, "But, Lord, why do you intend to show yourself to us and not to the world?"

²³Jesus replied, "If anyone loves me, he will obey my teaching. My Father will love him, and we will come to him and make our home with him. ²⁴He who does not love me will not obey my teaching. These

words you hear are not my own; they belong to the Father who sent me.

²⁵"All this I have spoken while still with you. ²⁶But the Counselor, the Holy Spirit, whom the Father will send in my name, will teach you all things and will remind you of everything I have said to you. ²⁷Peace I leave with you; my peace I give you. I do not give to you as the world gives. Do not let your hearts be troubled and do not be afraid.

²⁸"You heard me say, 'I am going away and I am coming back to you.' If you loved me, you would be glad that I am going to the Father, for the Father is greater than I. ²⁹I have told you now before it happens, so that when it does happen you will believe. ³⁰I will not speak with you much longer, for the prince of this world is coming. He has no hold on me, ³¹but the world must learn that I love the Father and that I do exactly what my Father has commanded me.

"Come now; let us leave.

15

"I am the true vine, and my Father is the gardener. ²He cuts off every branch in me that bears no fruit, while every branch that does bear fruit he prunes so that it will be even more fruitful. ³You are already clean because of the word I have spoken to you. ⁴Remain in me, and I will remain in you. No branch can bear fruit by itself; it must remain in the vine. Neither can you bear fruit unless you remain in me.

⁵"I am the vine; you are the branches. If a man remains in me and I in him, he will bear much fruit; apart from me you can do nothing. ⁶If anyone does not remain in me, he is like a branch that is thrown away and withers; such branches are picked up, thrown into the fire and burned. ⁷If you remain in me and my words

remain in you, ask whatever you wish, and it will be given you. [8]This is to my Father's glory, that you bear much fruit, showing yourselves to be my disciples.

[9]"As the Father has loved me, so have I loved you. Now remain in my love. [10]If you obey my commands, you will remain in my love, just as I have obeyed my Father's commands and remain in his love. [11]I have told you this so that my joy may be in you and that your joy may be complete. [12]My command is this: Love each other as I have loved you. [13]Greater love has no one than this, that he lay down his life for his friends. [14]You are my friends if you do what I command. [15]I no longer call you servants, because a servant does not know his master's business. Instead, I have called you friends, for everything that I learned from my Father I have made known to you. [16]You did not choose me, but I chose you and appointed you to go and bear fruit—fruit that will last. Then the Father will give you whatever you ask in my name. [17]This is my command: Love each other.

[18]"If the world hates you, keep in mind that it hated me first. [19]If you belonged to the world, it would love you as its own. As it is, you do not belong to the world, but I have chosen you out of the world. That is why the world hates you. [20]Remember the words I spoke to you: 'No servant is greater than his master.' If they persecuted me, they will persecute you also. If they obeyed my teaching, they will obey yours also. [21]They will treat you this way because of my name, for they do not know the One who sent me. [22]If I had not come and spoken to them, they would not be guilty of sin. Now, however, they have no excuse for their sin. [23]He who hates me hates my Father as well. [24]If I had not done among them what no one else did, they would not be guilty of sin. But now they have seen these miracles, and yet they have

hated both me and my Father. ²⁵But this is to fulfill what is written in their Law: 'They hated me without reason.'

²⁶"When the Counselor comes, whom I will send to you from the Father, the Spirit of truth who goes out from the Father, he will testify about me. ²⁷And you also must testify, for you have been with me from the beginning.

16

"All this I have told you so that you will not go astray. ²They will put you out of the synagogue; in fact, a time is coming when anyone who kills you will think he is offering a service to God. ³They will do such things because they have not known the Father or me. ⁴I have told you this, so that when the time comes you will remember that I warned you. I did not tell you this at first because I was with you.

⁵"Now I am going to him who sent me, yet none of you asks me, 'Where are you going?' ⁶Because I have said these things, you are filled with grief. ⁷But I tell you the truth: It is for your good that I am going away. Unless I go away, the Counselor will not come to you; but if I go, I will send him to you. ⁸When he comes, he will convict the world of guilt in regard to sin and righteousness and judgment: ⁹in regard to sin, because men do not believe in me; ¹⁰in regard to righteousness, because I am going to the Father, where you can see me no longer; ¹¹and in regard to judgment, because the prince of this world now stands condemned.

¹²"I have much more to say to you, more than you can now bear. ¹³But when he, the Spirit of truth, comes, he will guide you into all truth. He will not speak on his own; he will speak only what he hears, and he will tell you what is yet to come. ¹⁴He will bring glory to me by taking from what is mine and making it known to you.

[15]All that belongs to the Father is mine. That is why I said the Spirit will take from what is mine and make it known to you.

[16]"In a little while you will see me no more, and then after a little while you will see me."

[17]Some of his disciples said to one another, "What does he mean by saying, 'In a little while you will see me no more, and then after a little while you will see me,' and 'Because I am going to the Father'?" [18]They kept asking, "What does he mean by 'a little while'? We don't understand what he is saying."

[19]Jesus saw that they wanted to ask him about this, so he said to them, "Are you asking one another what I meant when I said, 'In a little while you will see me no more, and then after a little while you will see me'? [20]I tell you the truth, you will weep and mourn while the world rejoices. You will grieve, but your grief will turn to joy. [21]A woman giving birth to a child has pain because her time has come; but when her baby is born she forgets the anguish because of her joy that a child is born into the world. [22]So with you: Now is your time of grief, but I will see you again and you will rejoice, and no one will take away your joy. [23]In that day you will no longer ask me anything. I tell you the truth, my Father will give you whatever you ask in my name. [24]Until now you have not asked for anything in my name. Ask and you will receive, and your joy will be complete.

[25]"Though I have been speaking figuratively, a time is coming when I will no longer use this kind of language but will tell you plainly about my Father. [26]In that day you will ask in my name. I am not saying that I will ask the Father on your behalf. [27]No, the Father himself loves you because you have loved me and have believed that I came from God. [28]I came from the Father and

entered the world; now I am leaving the world and going back to the Father."

[29]Then Jesus' disciples said, "Now you are speaking clearly and without figures of speech. [30]Now we can see that you know all things and that you do not even need to have anyone ask you questions. This makes us believe that you came from God."

[31]"You believe at last!" Jesus answered. [32]"But a time is coming, and has come, when you will be scattered, each to his own home. You will leave me all alone. Yet I am not alone, for my Father is with me.

[33]"I have told you these things, so that in me you may have peace. In this world you will have trouble. But take heart! I have overcome the world."

17

After Jesus said this, he looked toward heaven and prayed:

"Father, the time has come. Glorify your Son, that your Son may glorify you. [2]For you granted him authority over all people that he might give eternal life to all those you have given him. [3]Now this is eternal life: that they may know you, the only true God, and Jesus Christ, whom you have sent. [4]I have brought you glory on earth by completing the work you gave me to do. [5]And now, Father, glorify me in your presence with the glory I had with you before the world began.

[6]"I have revealed you to those whom you gave me out of the world. They were yours; you gave them to me and they have obeyed your word. [7]Now they know that everything you have given me comes from you. [8]For I gave them the words you gave me and they accepted them. They knew with certainty that I came from you, and they believed that you sent me. [9]I pray for them. I am not praying for the world, but for those you have

given me, for they are yours. [10]All I have is yours, and all you have is mine. And glory has come to me through them. [11]I will remain in the world no longer, but they are still in the world, and I am coming to you. Holy Father, protect them by the power of your name—the name you gave me—so that they may be one as we are one. [12]While I was with them, I protected them and kept them safe by that name you gave me. None has been lost except the one doomed to destruction so that Scripture would be fulfilled.

[13]"I am coming to you now, but I say these things while I am still in the world, so that they may have the full measure of my joy within them. [14]I have given them your word and the world has hated them, for they are not of the world any more than I am of the world. [15]My prayer is not that you take them out of the world but that you protect them from the evil one. [16]They are not of the world, even as I am not of it. [17]Sanctify them by the truth; your word is truth. [18]As you sent me into the world, I have sent them into the world. [19]For them I sanctify myself, that they too may be truly sanctified.

[20]"My prayer is not for them alone. I pray also for those who will believe in me through their message, [21]that all of them may be one, Father, just as you are in me and I am in you. May they also be in us so that the world may believe that you have sent me. [22]I have given them the glory that you gave me, that they may be one as we are one: [23]I in them and you in me. May they be brought to complete unity to let the world know that you sent me and have loved them even as you have loved me.

[24]"Father, I want those you have given me to be with me where I am, and to see my glory, the glory you have given me because you loved me before the creation of the world.

²⁵"Righteous Father, though the world does not know you, I know you, and they know that you have sent me. ²⁶I have made you known to them, and will continue to make you known in order that the love you have for me may be in them and that I myself may be in them."

18

When he had finished praying, Jesus left with his disciples and crossed the Kidron Valley. On the other side there was an olive grove, and he and his disciples went into it.

²Now Judas, who betrayed him, knew the place, because Jesus had often met there with his disciples. ³So Judas came to the grove, guiding a detachment of soldiers and some officials from the chief priests and Pharisees. They were carrying torches, lanterns and weapons.

⁴Jesus, knowing all that was going to happen to him, went out and asked them, "Who is it you want?"

⁵"Jesus of Nazareth," they replied.

"I am he," Jesus said. (And Judas the traitor was standing there with them.) ⁶When Jesus said, "I am he," they drew back and fell to the ground.

⁷Again he asked them, "Who is it you want?"

And they said, "Jesus of Nazareth."

⁸"I told you that I am he," Jesus answered. "If you are looking for me, then let these men go." ⁹This happened so that the words he had spoken would be fulfilled: "I have not lost one of those you gave me."

¹⁰Then Simon Peter, who had a sword, drew it and struck the high priest's servant, cutting off his right ear. (The servant's name was Malchus.)

¹¹Jesus commanded Peter, "Put your sword away! Shall I not drink the cup the Father has given me?"

¹²Then the detachment of soldiers with its commander and the Jewish officials arrested Jesus. They bound him ¹³and brought him first to Annas, who was the father-in-law of Caiaphas, the high priest that year. ¹⁴Caiaphas was the one who had advised the Jews that it would be good if one man died for the people.

¹⁵Simon Peter and another disciple were following Jesus. Because this disciple was known to the high priest, he went with Jesus into the high priest's courtyard, ¹⁶but Peter had to wait outside at the door. The other disciple, who was known to the high priest, came back, spoke to the girl on duty there and brought Peter in.

¹⁷"You are not one of his disciples, are you?" the girl at the door asked Peter.

He replied, "I am not."

¹⁸It was cold, and the servants and officials stood around a fire they had made to keep warm. Peter also was standing with them, warming himself.

¹⁹Meanwhile, the high priest questioned Jesus about his disciples and his teaching.

²⁰"I have spoken openly to the world," Jesus replied. "I always taught in synagogues or at the temple, where all the Jews come together. I said nothing in secret. ²¹Why question me? Ask those who heard me. Surely they know what I said."

²²When Jesus said this, one of the officials nearby struck him in the face. "Is this the way you answer the high priest?" he demanded.

²³"If I said something wrong," Jesus replied, "testify as to what is wrong. But if I spoke the truth, why did you strike me?" ²⁴Then Annas sent him, still bound, to Caiaphas the high priest.

²⁵As Simon Peter stood warming himself, he was asked, "You are not one of his disciples, are you?"

He denied it, saying, "I am not."

^{26}One of the high priest's servants, a relative of the man whose ear Peter had cut off, challenged him, "Didn't I see you with him in the olive grove?" ^{27}Again Peter denied it, and at that moment a rooster began to crow.

^{28}Then the Jews led Jesus from Caiaphas to the palace of the Roman governor. By now it was early morning, and to avoid ceremonial uncleanness the Jews did not enter the palace; they wanted to be able to eat the Passover. ^{29}So Pilate came out to them and asked, "What charges are you bringing against this man?"

^{30}"If he were not a criminal," they replied, "we would not have handed him over to you."

^{31}Pilate said, "Take him yourselves and judge him by your own law."

"But we have no right to execute anyone," the Jews objected. ^{32}This happened so that the words Jesus had spoken indicating the kind of death he was going to die would be fulfilled.

^{33}Pilate then went back inside the palace, summoned Jesus and asked him, "Are you the king of the Jews?"

^{34}"Is that your own idea," Jesus asked, "or did others talk to you about me?"

^{35}"Am I a Jew?" Pilate replied. "It was your people and your chief priests who handed you over to me. What is it you have done?"

^{36}Jesus said, "My kingdom is not of this world. If it were, my servants would fight to prevent my arrest by the Jews. But now my kingdom is from another place."

^{37}"You are a king, then!" said Pilate.

Jesus answered, "You are right in saying I am a king. In fact, for this reason I was born, and for this I came into the world, to testify to the truth. Everyone on the side of truth listens to me."

[38]"What is truth?" Pilate asked. With this he went out again to the Jews and said, "I find no basis for a charge against him. [39]But it is your custom for me to release to you one prisoner at the time of the Passover. Do you want me to release 'the king of the Jews'?"

[40]They shouted back, "No, not him! Give us Barabbas!" Now Barabbas had taken part in a rebellion.

19

Then Pilate took Jesus and had him flogged. [2]The soldiers twisted together a crown of thorns and put it on his head. They clothed him in a purple robe [3]and went up to him again and again, saying, "Hail, king of the Jews!" And they struck him in the face.

[4]Once more Pilate came out and said to the Jews, "Look, I am bringing him out to you to let you know that I find no basis for a charge against him." [5]When Jesus came out wearing the crown of thorns and the purple robe, Pilate said to them, "Here is the man!"

[6]As soon as the chief priests and their officials saw him, they shouted, "Crucify! Crucify!"

But Pilate answered, "You take him and crucify him. As for me, I find no basis for a charge against him."

[7]The Jews insisted, "We have a law, and according to that law he must die, because he claimed to be the Son of God."

[8]When Pilate heard this, he was even more afraid, [9]and he went back inside the palace. "Where do you come from?" he asked Jesus, but Jesus gave him no answer. [10]"Do you refuse to speak to me?" Pilate said. "Don't you realize I have power either to free you or to crucify you?"

[11]Jesus answered, "You would have no power over me if it were not given to you from above. Therefore the one who handed me over to you is guilty of a greater sin."

[12]From then on, Pilate tried to set Jesus free, but the Jews kept shouting, "If you let this man go, you are no friend of Caesar. Anyone who claims to be a king opposes Caesar."

[13]When Pilate heard this, he brought Jesus out and sat down on the judge's seat at a place known as the Stone Pavement (which in Aramaic is Gabbatha). [14]It was the day of Preparation of Passover Week, about the sixth hour.

"Here is your king," Pilate said to the Jews.

[15]But they shouted, "Take him away! Take him away! Crucify him!"

"Shall I crucify your king?" Pilate asked.

"We have no king but Caesar," the chief priests answered.

[16]Finally Pilate handed him over to them to be crucified.

So the soldiers took charge of Jesus. [17]Carrying his own cross, he went out to the place of the Skull (which in Aramaic is called Golgotha). [18]Here they crucified him, and with him two others—one on each side and Jesus in the middle.

[19]Pilate had a notice prepared and fastened to the cross. It read: JESUS OF NAZARETH, THE KING OF THE JEWS. [20]Many of the Jews read this sign, for the place where Jesus was crucified was near the city, and the sign was written in Aramaic, Latin and Greek. [21]The chief priests of the Jews protested to Pilate, "Do not write 'The King of the Jews,' but that this man claimed to be king of the Jews."

[22]Pilate answered, "What I have written, I have written."

[23]When the soldiers crucified Jesus, they took his clothes, dividing them into four shares, one for each of

them, with the undergarment remaining. This garment was seamless, woven in one piece from top to bottom.

²⁴"Let's not tear it," they said to one another. "Let's decide by lot who will get it."

This happened that the scripture might be fulfilled which said,

"They divided my garments among them
and cast lots for my clothing."

So this is what the soldiers did.

²⁵Near the cross of Jesus stood his mother, his mother's sister, Mary the wife of Clopas, and Mary Magdalene. ²⁶When Jesus saw his mother there, and the disciple whom he loved standing nearby, he said to his mother, "Dear woman, here is your son," ²⁷and to the disciple, "Here is your mother." From that time on, this disciple took her into his home.

²⁸Later, knowing that all was now completed, and so that the Scripture would be fulfilled, Jesus said, "I am thirsty." ²⁹A jar of wine vinegar was there, so they soaked a sponge in it, put the sponge on a stalk of the hyssop plant, and lifted it to Jesus' lips. ³⁰When he had received the drink, Jesus said, "It is finished." With that, he bowed his head and gave up his spirit.

³¹Now it was the day of Preparation, and the next day was to be a special Sabbath. Because the Jews did not want the bodies left on the crosses during the Sabbath, they asked Pilate to have the legs broken and the bodies taken down. ³²The soldiers therefore came and broke the legs of the first man who had been crucified with Jesus, and then those of the other. ³³But when they came to Jesus and found that he was already dead, they did not break his legs. ³⁴Instead, one of the soldiers pierced Jesus' side with a spear, bringing a sudden flow of blood

and water. [35]The man who saw it has given testimony, and his testimony is true. He knows that he tells the truth, and he testifies so that you also may believe. [36]These things happened so that the scripture would be fulfilled: "Not one of his bones will be broken," [37]and, as another scripture says, "They will look on the one they have pierced."

[38]Later, Joseph of Arimathea asked Pilate for the body of Jesus. Now Joseph was a disciple of Jesus, but secretly because he feared the Jews. With Pilate's permission, he came and took the body away. [39]He was accompanied by Nicodemus, the man who earlier had visited Jesus at night. Nicodemus brought a mixture of myrrh and aloes, about seventy-five pounds. [40]Taking Jesus' body, the two of them wrapped it, with the spices, in strips of linen. This was in accordance with Jewish burial customs. [41]At the place where Jesus was crucified, there was a garden, and in the garden a new tomb, in which no one had ever been laid. [42]Because it was the Jewish day of Preparation and since the tomb was nearby, they laid Jesus there.

20

Early on the first day of the week, while it was still dark, Mary Magdalene went to the tomb and saw that the stone had been removed from the entrance. [2]So she came running to Simon Peter and the other disciple, the one Jesus loved, and said, "They have taken the Lord out of the tomb, and we don't know where they have put him!"

[3]So Peter and the other disciple started for the tomb. [4]Both were running, but the other disciple outran Peter and reached the tomb first. [5]He bent over and looked in at the strips of linen lying there but did not go in. [6]Then Simon Peter, who was behind him, arrived and went into the tomb. He saw the strips of linen lying there, [7]as well

as the burial cloth that had been around Jesus' head. The cloth was folded up by itself, separate from the linen. [8]Finally the other disciple, who had reached the tomb first, also went inside. He saw and believed. [9](They still did not understand from Scripture that Jesus had to rise from the dead.)

[10]Then the disciples went back to their homes, [11]but Mary stood outside the tomb crying. As she wept, she bent over to look into the tomb [12]and saw two angels in white, seated where Jesus' body had been, one at the head and the other at the foot.

[13]They asked her, "Woman, why are you crying?"

"They have taken my Lord away," she said, "and I don't know where they have put him." [14]At this, she turned around and saw Jesus standing there, but she did not realize that it was Jesus.

[15]"Woman," he said, "why are you crying? Who is it you are looking for?"

Thinking he was the gardener, she said, "Sir, if you have carried him away, tell me where you have put him, and I will get him."

[16]Jesus said to her, "Mary."

She turned toward him and cried out in Aramaic, "Rabboni!" (which means Teacher).

[17]Jesus said, "Do not hold on to me, for I have not yet returned to the Father. Go instead to my brothers and tell them, 'I am returning to my Father and your Father, to my God and your God.'"

[18]Mary Magdalene went to the disciples with the news: "I have seen the Lord!" And she told them that he had said these things to her.

[19]On the evening of that first day of the week, when the disciples were together, with the doors locked for fear of the Jews, Jesus came and stood among them and said, "Peace be with you!" [20]After he said this, he showed

them his hands and side. The disciples were overjoyed when they saw the Lord.

[21]Again Jesus said, "Peace be with you! As the Father has sent me, I am sending you." [22]And with that he breathed on them and said, "Receive the Holy Spirit. [23]If you forgive anyone his sins, they are forgiven; if you do not forgive them, they are not forgiven."

[24]Now Thomas (called Didymus), one of the Twelve, was not with the disciples when Jesus came. [25]So the other disciples told him, "We have seen the Lord!"

But he said to them, "Unless I see the nail marks in his hands and put my finger where the nails were, and put my hand into his side, I will not believe it."

[26]A week later his disciples were in the house again, and Thomas was with them. Though the doors were locked, Jesus came and stood among them and said, "Peace be with you!" [27]Then he said to Thomas, "Put your finger here; see my hands. Reach out your hand and put it into my side. Stop doubting and believe."

[28]Thomas said to him, "My Lord and my God!"

[29]Then Jesus told him, "Because you have seen me, you have believed; blessed are those who have not seen and yet have believed."

[30]Jesus did many other miraculous signs in the presence of his disciples, which are not recorded in this book. [31]But these are written that you may believe that Jesus is the Christ, the Son of God, and that by believing you may have life in his name.

21

Afterward Jesus appeared again to his disciples, by the Sea of Tiberias. It happened this way: [2]Simon Peter, Thomas (called Didymus), Nathanael from Cana in Galilee, the sons of Zebedee, and two other disciples were together. ³"I'm going out to fish," Simon Peter told them, and they said, "We'll go with you." So they went out and got into the boat, but that night they caught nothing.

⁴Early in the morning, Jesus stood on the shore, but the disciples did not realize that it was Jesus.

⁵He called out to them, "Friends, haven't you any fish?"

"No," they answered.

⁶He said, "Throw your net on the right side of the boat and you will find some." When they did, they were unable to haul the net in because of the large number of fish.

⁷Then the disciple whom Jesus loved said to Peter, "It is the Lord!" As soon as Simon Peter heard him say, "It is the Lord," he wrapped his outer garment around him (for he had taken it off) and jumped into the water. ⁸The other disciples followed in the boat, towing the net full of fish, for they were not far from shore, about a hundred yards. ⁹When they landed, they saw a fire of burning coals there with fish on it, and some bread.

¹⁰Jesus said to them, "Bring some of the fish you have just caught."

¹¹Simon Peter climbed aboard and dragged the net ashore. It was full of large fish, 153, but even with so many the net was not torn. ¹²Jesus said to them, "Come and have breakfast." None of the disciples dared ask him, "Who are you?" They knew it was the Lord. ¹³Jesus came, took the bread and gave it to them, and did the same with the fish. ¹⁴This was now the third time Jesus appeared to his disciples after he was raised from the dead.

¹⁵When they had finished eating, Jesus said to Simon Peter, "Simon son of John, do you truly love me more than these?"